THE LAST OF THE BLACKFOLDERS

JIM FRASER

BALBOA.PRESS

A DIVISION OF HAY HOUSE

Balboa Press books may be ordered through booksellers or by contacting:

Balboa Press
A Division of Hay House
1663 Liberty Drive
Bloomington, IN 47403
www.balboapress.co.uk
UK TFN: 0800 0148647 (Toll Free inside the UK)
UK Local: 02036 956325 (+44 20 3695 6325 from outside the UK)

Because of the dynamic nature of the Internet, any web addresses or
links contained in this book may have changed since publication and
may no longer be valid. The views expressed in this work are solely those
of the author and do not necessarily reflect the views of the publisher,
and the publisher hereby disclaims any responsibility for them.

The author of this book does not dispense medical advice or prescribe the use
of any technique as a form of treatment for physical, emotional, or medical
problems without the advice of a physician, either directly or indirectly. The
intent of the author is only to offer information of a general nature to help
you in your quest for emotional and spiritual well-being. In the event you use
any of the information in this book for yourself, which is your constitutional
right, the author and the publisher assume no responsibility for your actions.

Print information available on the last page.

ISBN: 978-1-9822-8139-7 (sc)
ISBN: 978-1-9822-8140-3 (e)

Balboa Press rev. date: 12/03/2021

I dedicate this book to my two sons Jamie and Rory and I would further like to mention a few names of people who have helped and inspired me with this mammoth task. Mary Sciascia, my old schoolteacher's niece for her inspiration and perseverance in getting me to write this book, now living in the U.S.A Douglas Yule a new friend I have made, Freda Newton and all at Loch Ness by Jacobite for her help and guidance. My delightful cousin Liz Bligh, Ruaridh Hannah, Emma Foster and Dan, Maggie Third my hairdresser. All the nurses and surgeons from the plastic surgery ward at Raigmore Hospital, Lady Provost Helen Carmichael and many others too many to mention Finally a special mention to my two greatest buddies of many moons Andy Kennedy and Jimmy Paterson

Introduction

The manuscript for this book has been with the publishers for well over a year now due to this horrendous covid virus, which has practically brought the whole world to a standstill, and quite a lot has happened during that time. My dear sister Nan, with whom I am sure you are well familiar with by now passed away in June 2020 at Highview nursing home. Poor Nan came to a sad end as she suffered from dementia, that very cruel disease which robbed her of practically all her senses. I watched her slowly deteriorate, although I was the only one she knew or recognised right almost to the end. The bond that we formed from our latter days in Blackfold seemed to come to the fore, despite all our earlier childhood indifferences.

Of course, as the covid virus started to bite really hard all visits to the nursing home were suspended. Then one day in early June 2020 I got a phone call from the nursing home informing me that Nan had taken a bad turn and advised me that I should come to see her. I would be allowed, provided I would wear all the appropriate protective clothing. When I eventually arrived at the nursing home the nurses told me that they didn't expect Nan to go on much longer and when I saw her lying on her bed, I realised she was nearing the last mile. She was in a deep sleep, but as I gently stroked her pale grey forehead, which was once so brown and weather-beaten, her eyes flickered at the sound of my voice, and I knew that she knew I was there at her side. I recited some of her favourite scripture as best as I could remember and a shadow of a smile fluttered over her face. Memories in the confines of my mind, which had been locked away for so long came to view and I sadly left my dear sister, knowing that this would probably be the last time I would see her this side of Heaven.

Next morning, I got the dreaded but expected phone call informing me that Nan had passed away peacefully in the early hours, but she wasn't on her own. One of the nurses stayed by her side right to the end.

The funeral was a quiet affair due to the covid restrictions on attendance. Nevertheless, a beautifully uplifting service was conducted by the Rev David Scott. We stood there in that little churchyard in the shadow of a giant yew tree which stood like a silent witness for the many who would have otherwise attended, spreading its mighty branches, shielding the few that were there. Nan is buried in a little country graveyard at Bona on the shores of Loch Ness. Buried alongside my dear mum and dad and Isobel Anne my infant sister. As the burial ground is now full, there is not even room for a wee man like me and now i am truly The Last of the Blackfolders.

Brought up in the heights of Blackfold where the pine trees seem to touch the sky and where one could go days without seeing a stranger, this wonderfully strange environment has, as one would suspect shaped my character and my life. A lot of people and especially the children at the Dochgarroch primary school which i attended looked on me as someone totally different to them. This strange, lonely character arriving late for school most mornings after a daily trek of some three miles, without the teacher giving me a telling off seemed to hold them in awe of me. I suppose I am and always will be a sort of laid-back character, in fact someone once told me if i was any more laid back i would be horizontal. I spent a good deal of my life working on the family crofts I left school at the grand old age of fifteen and started work on the Dochfour estate forestry department. I Left the forestry due to a serious back injury and got a job with Ross leighs garage as a costing clerk. I Left there and then followed a string of self-employed work, including erecting deer and cattle fences all over the Highlands' some seasonal work as a ghillie on Mullardoch estate during the stag shooting season.

I Travelled across the Irish sea to Belfast and re-letting houses to accommodate workers for the Harland and Wolfe ship building yard. I met so many characters in my life I thought it would be a shame for them to be forgotten and disappear into the mists of time and having been spurred on by a few people I thought I would put pen to paper, hence this book. Today and now in my twilight years I live right next to the old Dochgarroch hall, now a beautiful restaurant An Talla, where I wander down for a coffee and a bit of craic.

So that's about all i have to say for myself at the moment, the rest you'll find out in the hidden pages of this book. Happy reading and take care, Jim.

This is the story of my life on a remote croft in the Scottish Highlands and then a wee bit further afield.

I was born at Rose Cottage, Davies Square,

Inverness, just behind the Black Bull Inn. The year was 1944 the month was August, but the day, well I'm not too sure. You see my mum told me I was born on the 4th of August and so it says on all my documents, driving license, Insurance card etc., with the exception of my birth certificate.

One day I was rummaging about in an old Welsh dresser out in the barn and I came across my ID card and birth lines, clearly stating I was born on the 3rd August 1944. I ran into the old croft house and said "look mum, I wasn't born on the 4th it was the 3rd of August". She looked at me in a coy sort of way and said "ah! I always thought it was the 4th".

My mum was a great one for the Royal family, especially the Queen Mother and I got myself to thinking. The Queen Mother was born on the 4th of August and my mum was so proud of the fact that I shared my birthday with her and I am pretty certain that was the reason for the change. So, on the radio every year on the 4th of August the national anthem would play and mum would say "oh! It's the Queen Mother's birthday today, the same day as yours James".

My Mum was very proud of the fact that her mum, my grannie's cousin was Lady in waiting to the Queen Mother during part of the war years. She was a miss Maclean who resided at the Dores Inn, just outside of Inverness. Seemingly Miss Maclean could no longer stand the blitz, and she decided to head back home, despite pleadings from the Queen Mother to stay.

The Queen Mother would often pop in for a visit on her way to the castle of May.

My mum lived in Brown Street when she was young, along with my granny and grandad and her brother and sister. Although her stepdad my grandad was very seldom at home, he was a seafaring man. I 'll tell you all about him a bit further along. That in itself is a long story.

Mum went to the Merkinch school a fact she was very proud of. When she was growing up, she used to visit her aunt Belle who had a croft at Lower Dunain. This developed into a very close friendly relationship between the two of them. Aunty Belle lived with her brother Calum and a boarded-out man Jack Brown who was a poor soul, he couldn't speak properly, nowadays he would have been classed as having very severe learning difficulties.

Aunty Belle was such a friendly lovely woman, the teapot was always on the go, in-between the yarns and sometimes she would take out her old melodeon, kept together by sticky paper and plasters.

There were a lot of little crofts around at that time, quite a nice wee community but sadly about the time of the clearances a lot of the crofters immigrated to the USA, Canada, Australia and New Zealand.

One of the houses just down from Aunty Belle was still inhabited by an old spinster called Joey, her old house is still called after her.

Mum and the other kids would go down at nights, knock on the door and run away just to annoy her.

Rabbits were all over the place during this time and of course with the rabbits came fleas and I mean fleas scores and scores of the little blighters. If you think midges are bad you should try sleeping in a bed infested with fleas.

The fleas would come into everyone's house on dead rabbits killed for the pot as well as on cats and dogs. All the cats would have a row of fleas along each ear. Mum used to tell us laughing that her and the other kids would peer in the window and there would be Joey sitting in front of a big roaring fire with her vest off, looking for fleas, there was great knack in catching them you first had to pin them either between two pieces of clothing or skin and very slowly uncover them or they would jump some two or three feet away. They were so hard you had to crush them between your thumb and fingernail. I bet it passed many a lonely night for poor Joey.

But fleas were certainly not a sign of dirt, they were just part of country living, even the gentry had them and maybe more so, with all the hunting and shooting they all did.

Next to the croft at Lower Dunain was a very large rabbit warren, there was a five-foot rabbit fence all the way round and at frequent intervals there were one-way entrance traps. The rabbits could rush the little doors to get in, but they couldn't get out. This led to the enormous population of rabbits. I remember my dad telling me at one rabbit shoot, the rabbits were piled so high against the fence that they were jumping over the dead and wounded ones. One of the shooters handed his gun to my dad and said "I'm going home I've had enough; this is not sport its downright slaughter.

Outside of the warren there were numerous other little squares with these one-way traps, which can still be seen to this day. Mum was an expert rabbit trapper she had this beautiful big rough. Black and tan collie called Kruger or Crouger and together they were a formidable pair. The game keepers and trappers used to see mum going home with a haul for her aunty Belle and they would say "I wish we could catch rabbits like that wee lassie". Aunty Belle and Calum would sell the rabbits to the butcher, which would pay for the groceries, a packet of Calum's favourite biscuits or "bistets" as mum would say he said. Sometimes there would be enough left over to get a wee half bottle of whisky

As mum grew up, she divided her time between home Rose Cottage and Lower Dunain, she had a great fancy for the nursing as she left school and applied for several jobs, but there were never any replies. Some time later on she found out that a good few of her applications had been accepted and some were very good jobs but her mum had hidden the letters, she said to her mum when she found the letters "that was an awful thing to do to me" to which her mum replied "oh! Jessie, I just didn't want you to go away" I don't suppose any of us want our children to go away if we are honest with each other.

So, one of the letters she had found was a successful application for a maid at Pitmain lodge, and it was there that she would meet her lifetime pal May Spencer, who I think came from Sussex. Mum used to reminisce fondly of her exploits with May. Sneaking in and out of the lodge at all hours and going to the Northern meeting balls, where they were called on for duty.

When mum went home to Rose Cottage on her days off, she found a quite hostile environment. Grandad would make one of his rare appearances, home from sea and she found she could no longer live there. Or to put it another way she no longer felt safe there

On returning to Pitmain after the weekend May said to mum "why don't you come with me to London there is plenty of work there and they are very keen on Scottish girls, especially ones from the Highlands. So, they said farewell to Pitmain and headed south for the bright lights of London.

After a short while mum was to find herself on her own. May had met an R.A.F service man and had developed a serious relationship so her and my mum said a very sorrowful farewell to each other at the Leicester Square underground and it would be a long, long time before they would see each other again.

So now mum was left all alone in London, she had been very dubious about big posh houses because her mum, my granny had told her a story about what happened to her when she was in service at a big house in London where she worked at as a maid when she was young. My granny was cleaning out one of the bedrooms in this big house,' she opened the wardrobe door and a body fell out, she ran screaming, terrified out of the house and never went back.

With this in mind my mum went for her first interview, and this is exactly the way she told it to me. She said "James, "I went up to this large doorway and rang the doorbell, a well-dressed lady answered the door and said," you must be Jessie, come in the lady of the house is expecting you". She led my mother into this large rather gloomy drawing room and introduced her to this lady of the house. My mums voice broke into a whisper as she described this person. "Oh! my gosh 'she said, "she was like a man, great big hands and teeth", she was sure it was a man dressed as a woman.

My mum was given the job as a so-called house maid and was to start first thing the next morning. When she got out, she was a wee bit disorientated, so she took some advice her old pal May had given her before they parted. Always ask a policeman for help don't trust anyone else whilst in London. So, she approached this policeman and asked if he could guide her to her lodgings in Leicester square. The policeman gave her directions and then said "Oh! By the way where did you come from" my mum turned around and pointed to the big house. The policeman looked at my mum and said "look dear don't go near that house ever again, it's an evil wicked house. There is many a girl that went there and never came out, it's under investigation at the moment'. I was young at the time and I didn't know that what my mum was trying to tell me was, that this house, a bad house was probably a brothel, so she ran all the way home and never looked back.

Mum then applied for and got a job as a housekeeper with a very nice, well to do elderly couple who had a big house in Regency Square.

She loved her job and this lovely couple were so very kind and good to her and she was so content for a good few months. She must have been keeping in touch with home for one day she received a telegram telling her she would have to return home as her uncle John was seriously ill and there was no-one else to look after him. Uncle John had a croft in which he lived by himself way, way up in the hills at Blackfold some 1,000 feet above sea level.

My mum explained to the couple who were bitterly disappointed and begged her to stay. The couple had no family and took such a liking to my mum (mind you that wouldn't be hard, practically everyone she met fell in love with her) that they told her if you stay, we will leave all this to you, the house and the large walled garden. My mum always told me "I could have been a lady with fancy long nails, gingham dresses, lovely court shoes and all that goes with it". Then she gave a deep sigh and a wee laugh, "look at me now James, I've got fancy rags and gingham sleeves for stockings and an old canvas bag apron. People didn't know that I was once in London and not just a green country lassie from the hills". If ever mum went to town which wasn't very often, my last words to her were always "watch yourself crossing the streets now".

So, mum said a sad tearful farewell to the lovely old

couple and told them she would try and return someday to look after them when things were sorted out at home.

So, mum returned to the Highlands to look after her uncle John who lived on this remote croft at Wester Blackfold. Uncle John was seriously ill and stricken with age but he still had most of his faculties about him. Blackfold was a far cry from the bright lights of London, goodbye electric light, flushing toilets, baths and running water, but my mum never complained, she always said "I was put on this earth for a purpose" and she looked on this nursing of John Blackfold as one of her purposes.

After a few months Uncle John had to be admitted to the Royal Northern Infirmary where they had all the facilities to look after him, that my mum never had. Then came the night Uncle John lay on his death bed. He was sucking on a large pan drop my mum told me laughing, he took it out of his mouth and said "Here Jessie you have it, I won't finish it I'm going home" Then he gathered all the nurses around his bed and thanked them all for their kindness. He then turned to mum and said "Jessie, I'm going home to be with the Lord, the angels are coming for me, I can hear them singing, can you hear them?" My mum said she could hear them and with that he closed his eyes and passed out of this world to be with the Lord. My mum said she had never seen such a peaceful death bed.

Before I go much further, I must tell you a wee bit about my dad. He was a good man but he was very, very hard on me. Nothing I did was ever right, no matter how hard I tried. My sister Nan was his big favourite and everyone knew this, friends, neighbours and relatives.

One day I recall my cousin Kenny saying to him "Don't be so hard on poor James, he's only a boy". Dad just replied with a grunt and the usual "ach, be quiet mun". I always waited and expected my dad to change and be a bit more sympathetic and kinder to me but alas he never did, indeed if anything he was getting much harder. I'm sorry folks I'm just telling you the way it was. My Uncle Kenny told me later, although not condoning it "I can't really blame your dad for being as hard on you for he was brought up by his uncle Willie who was a renowned hard man, hit first and ask questions later. I heard it said that he could put a bottle of whisky to his head and down it in a one. I somehow think this may have been a half bottle, but I'm sure it was a bottle I heard them talking about. So, I can well imagine what sort of a life my dad had with his uncle.

My dad's dad James Fraser came from Bowmore in Islay and he moved to the Highlands to seek work where he gained a position as gamekeeper forester with Dochfour estate. It wasn't long before he met and fell in love with Isabella and they married at Huntly Street according to the format of the Free church on the thirteenth day of May nineteen hundred and ten. 13/05/1910.

The first world war or the Great war as it became known broke out in 1914 and my grandad was called up and he joined The Queens own Cameron Highlanders and was drafted abroad to fight for our country. During this time my dad's mum, my granny had developed goitre a throat cancer with a very poor prognosis and she wasn't given long to live. Her dad had passed away and this left her mum my great grandmother to look after her. As her health rapidly deteriorated my grandad was given special leave to visit his wife. He returned home late June 1917 and was present at her beloved wife's bedside to see her pass away and into the mansion prepared for her as promised by Christ. By all accounts she was a lovely shy, God fearing person who doted on her wee son Alexander (my dad) who was only 7 years old at her death. It was a sad, sad day indeed especially for my grandad that day of the 4th of July 1917.

They carried her coffin over the hills along the hills along the old bridle path, a path she often played on amongst the heather when she was a wee lassie to the Wee Free church graveyard at Bona.

After just a few days of mourning my grandad had to return once more to the horrific scenes and trenches in Arras, Flanders and Ypres. He gave his mother-in-law a huge hug and lifted his wee son in his arms, gave him a long warm embrace and said goodbye. That would be the last time my father would ever see his dad. It was a long sad walk Ballymore to the Inverness train station, walking through the lovely heather clad hills, with the scent of the bog myrtle lingering on his clothes. I'm sure the peewits or lapwings would be calling a farewell tune, a sound he was so used to hearing, and loved so much on his many days in the hills.

So, my grandad returned to the horrors of the great war, he had come through it mostly unscathed, but that all changed eight months later as the German bullets ripped into him, killing him and many others on that fateful day 28th March 1918, he was just 37 years old.

I don't know if my grandads' body was ever recovered but I've been handed down his tunic buttons which would suggest he was found. I would have loved dearly to have taken him home and laid him to rest with his darling wife in the little graveyard at Bona. My grandmothers grave is overshadowed by a mighty giant yew tree, looking over it as if it were a great guardian angel.

So that left my dad with no mum or dad at just 7 years old and he was now to be looked after by his granny, a very strict Free Church woman. I often wondered if she, my great grandmother foresaw the deaths of her daughter and son in law as she was gifted with the second sight, I'll extend on that a little later on.

GV RI

HE whom this scroll commemorates was numbered among those who, at the call of King and Country, left all that was dear to them, endured hardness, faced danger, and finally passed out of the sight of men by the path of duty and self-sacrifice, giving up their own lives that others might live in freedom. Let those who come after see to it that his name be not forgotten.

S/22864, PRIVATE, James FRASER

7th Battalion,
Queen's Own Cameron Highlanders
Killed in action, France & Flanders, 28/03/18

Born: Inverness, Inverness-Shire, Enlisted: Kiltarlity, Inverness-Shire , Residence: Kiltarlity,

In Memory of

Private

James Fraser

22864, 7th Bn., Cameron Highlanders who died on 28 March 1918 Age 37

Son of Jessie and the late James Fraser; husband of the late Isabella McDonald Fraser.

Remembered with Honour
Arras Memorial

Commemorated in perpetuity by
the Commonwealth War Graves Commission

After my father lost his mum and dad he was as I have just written initially brought up by his granny a very strict Wee Free. By all accounts a kind extremely disciplinary woman. I got just a brief insight into her life through my dads' lifetime that Johnny Cooper, who lived in Paisley and holidayed often at Ballymore. He told me he was there when the letter came from the war department informing the next of kin that my dad's dad had been killed at Ypres. He said all the women were crying and my dad was just a wee boy, blue eyes, blonde curly hair running about not understanding the contents of the letter. Johnny said if my dad was out playing and he came near the house he used to say to him "is she in" those three words said a lot.

Every sabbath dad was sent to the Free church some three miles over the hill along the old bridle path to Bona. On his return after the service his granny would ask him what the sermon was all about. He was often made to memorise passages of scripture which he never forgot and he used to make me recite them and I can still remember them to this day. JOHN 3;16;17

For God so loved the world, that he gave his only begotten son, that whosoever believeth in him should not perish, but have everlasting life. For God sent not his Son into the world; to condemn the world, but that the world through him might be saved.

JOHN 14:1:2:3

'Let not your heart be troubled; ye believe in God, believe also in me. In my father's house are many mansions; if it were not so, I would have told you. I go to prepare a place for you. And if I go and prepare a place for you, I will come again and receive you unto myself, that where I am, there ye may be also.

JOHN 14:6

Jesus saith unto him, I am the way the truth and the life, no man cometh unto the father but by me.

Just before his grandad died," he was called red Rory," he sported a great bushy red beard. My dad would be sent down to the estate farm almost two miles away with the milk flagon so that his grandad would have the top of the milk for his broze. Then he would have to walk to the Inverness Royal Academy, a good five miles walk each day. I used to have to walk two and half miles each way to school but that was nothing compared to what he had to do. According to my dad's pal Johnny Cooper dad loved school, it was a welcome release from all the rigours and discipline of home. Johnny was a very Learned man; he was headmaster in a school in Paisley and he told me that dad stuck into his lessons and ended up becoming dux of the academy ahead of pupils much older than he. He cried uncontrollably when the time came for him to leave, he so much wanted to stay on, but in those days, there were no bursaries and if you couldn't afford to buy books, one had to leave. The headmaster visited his grandmother at Ballymore, imploring her to get Alex to stay, he could have been a lawyer, banker, teacher. Who knows but she just could not afford the expense?

I've lost count of the times my dad said to me "stick

in at your lessons boy, I wish I had the chance". Sort of ironic words in a way as I never had time to do my homework, he used to drag me out to work at nights, with these words ringing in my ears "we were taught all our lessons in class, we never got homework".

Dads' grandmother was noted throughout the whole of Blackfold and beyond for her gift of the second sight, she could foresee future events well in advance. I remember my dad telling us that when he was a wee boy, he would be walking along the Blackfold road to Ballymore and his grandmother would suddenly stop and say "stand to the side Alex there's a funeral coming". She would stand there and name everyone who passed, she would say to dad, there's Johnny, Mary and so on. My dad said he never saw or heard anything, but he was very frightened. The hairs on the back of his neck used to stand up Then sure enough in a few days there would be a death and the same funeral that had already been seen would take place

(Above Grandad, Granny and Dad.
Below Grandad cabin Ballymore)

The people who lived in old John Blackfolds house would tell us that just before a death you would often hear the lid of the old clothes chest open and slam shut. This was the chest where the Sunday best and funeral clothes were kept. Not many people ventured out after dark at Blackfold. Indeed, if visitors overstayed and darkness overtook them, they would usually stay till the morning. Shortly after my dad leaving school, his grandmother passed away leaving my dad on his own, but his uncle Willie sort of looked after him. I don't know how he survived. As Willie was a renowned hard, hard man a highly seasoned drinker and a temper to match.

(Dad, Uncle Willie and Ned the horse)

My mum told me that my dad was left a big house in Ballifeary but he was forced to sell it to pay for the drinks bill and other debts his uncle Willie had left).

I don't know when Uncle Willie died but around about then my dad met and started courting my mum and eventually, they got married on the 24th June 1936. My mum was brought up church of England and was confirmed in the Inverness Cathedral. My dad was brought up strictly Free Church completely opposing beliefs so they both agreed to have their wedding in a hotel. I can't remember which one. But it was a proper wedding with a minister officiating. As I am the only one now living who can recall all these events, there has to be a wee, just a wee bit of guess work.

Mum and dad went of their honeymoon to Glasgow, where the great Commonwealth exhibition was on at the time. Mum used to tell me as she burst out laughing, that dads Uncle Kenny said "I think I'll come with you, I'd love to see the exhibition". Dad said "aye Kenny that'll be ok". I bet he was as welcome as a fart in a space suit, as Billy Connelly once said.

They returned from their honeymoon in Glasgow to live in John Blackfolds old house and croft.

Then on the 4th of March 1939 mum gave birth to a baby girl Isobel Ann, who sadly passed away on the 26th May 1939 just two months and twenty-two days, she died of pneumonia. My mum always blamed the cold house for her death there were no heating at all till the open fire was lit. the cold biting winter winds created Arctic conditions, I remember this cold oh so well, nothing like what the cold feels like in the Lowlands.

My sister Jessie-Ann was born on the 24th May 1940

my mum giving birth I think in Culduthel hospital a much more friendly warmer environment.

Then later on my mum fell pregnant with little old me and as I said winters back then, especially high up as Blackfold were very severe. So, in view of this she moved down for a short time to be with her mum, my grandmother who lived in Inverness at Rose Cottage, Davis square with her two Aunts, just behind the old Black Bull Inn and it was there I was born on the 3rd/4th August 1944.

Just prior to my birth my dad applied for a farm job as grieve at Meikle Ussie on the Black Isle to which he was successful. World war 2 was raging at the time and the M.O.D were going around the country recruiting men to fight the war. Younne Cameron who owned the farm told the officials that he could not work the farm without my dad, especially with all his experience and of course the country needed and indeed depended on the farmers to produce as much food as possible to support the war effort and he was excused.

So, my mum, dad, Nan, my grandmother and I left for Meikle Ussie and the farming life. My mum told me a few stories about our short stay there. We shared a semi-detached house with one of the farm workers and there was a cupboard door joining the two houses which could be opened. Things were starting to go missing and my mum would look out to the washing line of her neighbours and see some of her London fashion clothes, blowing in the wind, then amongst other things her diamond engagement ring went missing. My mum had had enough, by his time and she was all for calling the police in, but my dad persuaded her not to as he didn't want to cause a fuss and lose the farm worker his job. So, he boarded the door up and I think that put an end to the stealing.

It is a strange thing one's memory, one can go way back in time and remember certain things and yet not remember what one had for dinner yesterday.

I was two when we were left Meikle Ussie so I must have been around that age when our house went on fire. I can remember my mum cradling me in her arms and carrying me down a steep stair. When she reached the door, she couldn't touch the steel doorknob it was red hot, but I remember her wrapping her apron around it and managing to get out.

My dad came rushing in from the field where he was ploughing and mu mum used to always tell us laughing, he was shouting "the pipes, oh the pipes" my dad's bag pipes and he rushed in and rescued them. The pipes were obviously very important to him. Probably the only link he had left with his late dad. I am no longer in possession of my dad's pipes which I find so very, very sad as my sister Nan has given them away, but when I asked her she said on no I would never have given the bagpipes away, especially with their history

The woman who stayed next door to us who was stealing things used to say to mum as she weighed up her lovely clothes and painted nails," aye Jessie there'll come a day when you go back to the croft, you'll not be dressed like that, you'll be just like me old rags and bachles of shoes" and oh boy how right she proved to be.

The war had ended and mum and dad, Nan and I headed back to Blackfold.

John Blackfolds old croft house was a stone built

but and ben, just a wooden partition separating the two rooms. There was an earthen floor a big open fireplace against the wall and a cast iron crook hanging from the chimney which was used for hanging the big heavy cast iron kettle. There was no running water in the house, it had all to be carried from a well about a quarter of a mile away on the moor. There was a burn flowing past the house but it was not very suitable for drinking.

Having no electricity mum did all her cooking on the fire. She would build up a fire with a pile of sticks and place the pan full of tatties on top and then go outside to do some work on the croft. Quite often she would come in and find the sticks had burned away and subsided and the pan of tatties would be coped over almost putting the fire out. But she got there in the end. Oops Miss MacFayden always taught us never to start a sentence with but!

Mum used to make besoms or brooms out of the broom, brushes to sweep the earth floor out with. She made good pot scrubbers out of heather, which were as good as, if not better that the ones you can buy today.

My dad got good part time work away from the croft on Dochfour estate in the forestry department. We had a big Clydesdale mare with a beautiful white blaze down the fronts of her head and face, she was called Sally a lovely docile beast and she was used for dragging logs out of the forest to the roadside for transportation to the sawmill and firewood for the big house. Mum used to come along to help sometimes, as the big Diston cross cut saw needed two people one on each end, when the logs were large. Of course, mum could put her hand to everything, she was an excellent axe person or hatchett as she called it. I think there was a bit of red Indian blood there somewhere, maybe that explains the Red Indians or more properly native Americans as being my favourite race, I would have loved to have lived with them. I remember the house at Blackfold being bitterly cold, sometimes going to bed with our clothes on, yes and the big army coats on top of a mountain of blankets.

The glass in the upstairs west room had been broken and fallen out, dad couldn't afford a new window pane so he patched it up with rabbit netting and cardboard. You could hear the wind whistling through the gaps and Nan used to terrify me by saying "oooh oooh, listen to the ghosties outside whistling to get in. They're going to catch you". I was terrified and I would try to bury myself even further into the pile of blankets. It's a wonder I got any sleep at all waiting for the ghosty to come in. Sometimes in a gale the powdery snow would blow in through the cracks in the cardboard and there would be a wee snowdrift on the foot of my bed. Its little wonder poor Isobel Ann my wee sister caught pneumonia.

We had a lot of days off school in the winter. The snowdrifts were much higher in those days, for some reason. I remember my mum opening the door and there was a snowdrift right up over the house. It was an awful job getting to the well for water, even finding the well was some job with the snow being so deep. My dad had to plough his way through snow drifts to make his way to work at the saw mill leaving us at home to keep the home fire burning so to speak.

The byre where we kept the cows, stirks and stots (the younger cattle) and the stable were about a quarter of a mile away along the road and my mum would have to carry water into them from a nearby burn. Then she would have to milk the cows and pail feed the calves then muck the byre out. There was always plenty of milk left over and she would make crowdy, which was nothing like the stuff you can buy in the shops today. Sometimes she would make cheese, but most often butter. My dad used to love the buttermilk so much so that I never got a chance to taste it. Tatties and milk was quite a common diet for us, good mealy Kerrs Pinks and Golden Wonders made a great meal.

I remember one very severe winter, the roads were blocked by snowdrifts and Nan and I had caught the chickenpox, poor mum caught it as well and also developed shingles, on their own bad enough, but together very serious.

Dr McKinnon managed to trudge through the snow mid-afternoon before the drifting started. He examined mum and told us that she would have to be admitted to Cuduthel Hospital right away. He said he would arrange an ambulance.

Shortly after a wind got up and the snow started to drift. Nan said good, the ambulance won't get through and take mum away, we both didn't want her to go. My father had made an old wooden drag snow plough which he had harnessed Sally the mare onto and went back and fore several times along the top of the hill where the drifts were worse in an effort to keep the road open. Some of the neighbours, two I think joined in with their shovels and eventually the ambulance arrived. I remember it being stuck at our house for a good while.

Mum told me afterward that she had made a lovely

rabbit stew and she was so looking forward to it, but then the ambulance came and she had no time to eat it.

Dad had to look after Nan and I. I wasn't looking forward to this at all at all. We were bed ridden for a while and he used to come in with this big jar of calamine lotion, it was like ice when he dabbed it on and he would say "keep still loon what are you shivering at'.' The stable diet then was broze. We always had broze for breakfast and mum used to give us syrup with it and sometimes, only sometimes Nestles condensed milk. But dad never put sugar on the broze just a big dodd of butter slapped on top. I used to lie and watch it slowly melt away like a great iceberg on top of a mountain. I really couldn't eat it all, it was nothing like mums, so I used to call Mona the wee collie bitch that we had through to the bedroom and quietly give it to her. Dad would come through after for the bowls and say "gosh you ate it all, you weren't long boy". Good old Mona. We lost her to strychnine poison later on at Dunain.

The Cooperative van used to come around once a week but could never get through the snow in the winter, then we had to trudge down to the bottom of the road, meet the van there and get the groceries. Then the long-haul home some 2 ½ miles all uphill. We also had paraffin to cart home in gallon cans to keep tilly lamps burning, they were a great source of light. Also, the old PYE radio ran on a big square dry battery and also a wet acid battery and that had to be charged about every fortnight. Scottish dance music was my and I think everyone's favourite program Jimmy Shand, Nan's favourite. Ian Powrie was my dad's favourite and mine was Jim Cameron and Bobby Macleod.

Between the battery and the paraffin, they were a burden on their own and the cap for the paraffin can was never a good fit, despite a bit of cloth and paper jammed around the cap. There was always a smell of paraffin of your clothes with all the splashing as you walked along.

Before the co-op van came around, Willie Allan the grocer was our only source of groceries, and cigarettes of course for dad. He used to smoke Capstan. But it was usually two or three in the morning before Willie came around. You see he liked a wee or not so wee dram and would fall asleep now and then.

One evening Willie came to the door in the snow and asked my dad if he could pull him out of the ditch with Sally the horse. My dad said "I'm not too keen to take the mare out as there is bad treacherous patches of ice, hidden beneath the snow. I'm not wanting the mare to break her leg and then what will we do". Dad said "by the way where are you stuck'?' to which Willie replied "the same place I was stuck in last week". Willie at last enticed my dad with a packet of Capstan cigarettes and he set out with the horse dragging the swingle-tree hitch behind. Dad hooked a thick chain to a secure point on Willies van which was a big heavy Albion. I never knew the tremendous power and grip that a horse could muster, A tractor would have just spun on the spot. But old Sally dug in and with a mighty pull the van was sitting on the hard road. Willie could hardly believe he was free so he thanked my dad took a huge swig out of his near empty bottle and went merrily on his way.

Our nearest next-door neighbour was Uncle John my late granny's brother, he was always referred to as

Johnny next door although he lived nigh on half a mile away. I always remember my sister Nan saying to me "See when Johnny next door is splitting firewood with the axe, you don't hear the sound for a second or two after". It's then I realised that sound took time to travel.

My mum told me that when Johnny was young, he was possibly the best dressed man in Inverness, for he was a tailor to trade. When he went to town, he was always immaculate from head to toe. He was always very eccentric; he had a great liking for long and fancy words that Nan and I did not understand.

Mum used to send Nan and I along with the grocery basket and a list to save her waiting up for Willie Allan the grocer. She knew that Johnny usually didn't mind staying up late. One night we went along with the basket and Johnny was not on good tune, he said to Nan and I "I'm not staying up late tonight you can get your own groceries", he was poking away at the fire, the poker was seldom out of his hand. Then he came out with what must have been annoying him." See that horse of yours, tell your dad to keep her on his own property, I hung up my washing out to dry and she chewed the backside out of my new drawers I had just bought last week". We stayed a little while longer and just as we were leaving, he said "ok just leave your basket but I hope Willie Allan is not as late as last week". Seemingly Willie had fallen asleep at the wheel and his van was blocking the road. Along came the patrol car and the policeman opened the door and Willie fell onto the road. The cold air and the short sleep had sobered Willie up and the policeman gave him a hand back onto the cab and gave him a telling off and told him to be on his way, so he was extra late that night.

About a good half mile in the opposite direction to the west lived an elderly couple, the woman was known to everyone just as granny Fraser. She was a very kind gracious soul, she quite often made home baking and she must have known that Nan and I got very little in the way of sweets or cakes, so sometimes you would see this wee figure in the distance coming along the road carrying a tray with a lovely white tea towel covering her baking. She had scones and I think pancakes but what I will never forget was her iced gingerbread and thatched with lashings of pink icing, I can still taste it yet. Next house along there were several occupants the last I remember was Mr Salvadori who had the wee shop on Greg Street, another person who must have felt sorry for us. One Christmas he came to the door with the best present we ever got. One of those large jars they used to have on the shop shelves full of fruit gums. What a lovely gentleman never forgot him for that. I also remember he had a most beautiful daughter.

(A picture I have drawn of Maggie, Lexy and Ellie)

Now I come to my favourite characters. Just about half a mile along the road from us lived three elderly sisters. Maggie, Lexy and Ellie Fraser. They lived in an old rundown wooden shack. Goodness knows how it got there it looked as if it had been there forever right beside the track of the edge of the old Blackfold forest and bordering with Blairnahenachrie, a place noted in the geological chronicles for its garnet marbles You could see the cattle grazing through the cracks in the wooden walls and every year March gales would rip the felt off. There wasn't much body in the wood to hold the felt tacks.

Two relations of the sisters both head teachers at Paisley and Bridge of Weir visited every year. John and Margaret Cooper were their names and they were also very close friends of my mum and dad. They were both a huge mine of information. I only wish I had taken more notice of the stories they told, but I do remember quite a few of them.

Johnny would get a large basin and kneel in it to spread his weight to prevent him falling through the roof and he would fix the new roles of felt as best he could, trying to find solid pieces of wood to hold the tacks. The sisters just like the cabin they lived in seemed to be there from time immemorial, no one in Blackfold could remember the place without them. They just seemed to always be there.

The sisters were renowned for their ghost stories and I think that is why I am so timid even to this day. It's not good for a young person to hear the sort of stories the sisters told. And they would swear on the bible that they were true and you know they were the sort of persons that would not and indeed could not tell lies. Maggie used to say "I better not tell any ghost stories when James and Nan are here", but I used to tug at mums' apron often and ask her to tell us some stories. Which I'll come to later.

Maggie and Lexy had a good few head of cattle, maybe twenty or so and quite often they would argue which one belonged to whom. It would get quite heated at times as all the beasts were black. Maggie would say "that's not my stirk its far too thin, that fat one over there by the shed is my one". Lexy would then say "don't you dare say my beast is too thin, you think you've got all the fat ones", but to tell you the truth they had some of the best if not the best cattle in the Highlands. They had the whole hill to graze on from Blackfold to a place called Blairnahenachrie where the ruins of a few old cottages could be seen, goodness knows who once lived there. The cottages were tucked away in the forest, several miles from nowhere. You certainly would not be going out for a ¼ of tea if you happened to run out.

Riggs the vet once said "Lexy doesn't know how many cows she has but she would know if there was one missing". Sometimes Lexy would time her shopping trip to town, to coincide with a visit from the vet and of course that would save her a taxi fare. Way back then the vets bill would be cheaper than a taxi.

It was always Lexy who went to town for the shopping, even though she had a cripple leg a result of a kick from one of her cows, but I'll bet she said it was one of Maggie's that kicked her. Lexy and Ellie always wore what appeared to be gabardine like coats on top of their long skirts and thick jerseys. Both wore berets, I never saw them without them even in their own house.

Maggie was a kind old soul but you had to keep on the right side of her, she always wrapped up just like my own mum. With about half a dozen jerseys, woolen pixie a scarf and a canvas bag, apron tied with an old piece of rope. She always had a switch in her hand which she used to drive the cattle and guide her ducks about.

Nobody hardly ever saw Nellie, a lifetime of living in Blackfold away from everywhere and everyone," you hardly ever saw anyone back in those days" had made her a very indeed mega shy person, Living in Blackfold then was like living on another planet, you could almost hear the silence at times.

When anyone came to the door or visited, Nellie would hide away in the bedroom. Nellie seemed to do most of the milking. The byre where she milked the cows was about seventy yards or so from their cabin. Nellie would check that the road was clear before scurrying to the byre milk pail in hand. When Nan and I were walking past on our way to school you would hear the milk from the cow squirting into the pail, but as soon as she heard our footsteps, she would stop milking. When we furtively looked back, you would see Nellie peering round the edge of the door.

Maggie used to invite mum, Nan and I along for a wee ceilidh round about Halloween.

What a feast Maggie would put on for us, all her home baking, she was so proud of scones with raspberry, bramble jam, oatcakes, crowdy. Homemade cheese and butter and then the ghost stories would start. The place and the atmosphere were just right. An old wooden cabin tucked into the edge of the forest, a bright full moon, a roaring woodburning stove and three old cronies telling their yarns.

They actually had better heating in that old cabin than we had. The woodburning stove and the tin chimney going out the gable end would be red hot. Lexy would occasionally go outside and splash a pail of water onto the wood to cool it down a wee bit. The wood nevertheless was protected by a large sheet of tin nailed on the back of the stove.

Lexy was somewhat different to Maggie. Looking back, I think she thought that all little boys were bad and making fun of her crippled leg and crooked back. She would threaten me with this story. How could I possibly ever forget it? She would say "you know what happens to bad boys" it was never bad little girls "there's a big bad wolf man up in the woods and he has a big axe" then she would stop and say "listen what's that noise, Oh yes I know what that noise is it's the big bad wolf man sharpening his axe, and he chops the bad boys heads off" again she would stop and say "listen can you hear the screams "I was absolutely terrified, I must have only been about seven or eight at the time.

One of the few if not only times I heard Nellie speak was one morning when Nan and I were walking to school. She had a lovely blue grey Persian cat called Feather which hardly anybody ever saw, a bit like Nellie herself. The cat was kept in all the time for fear of it running away. This morning Feather was sitting at the window and we stepped closer to get a better look, next minute the byre door swung open and Nellie shouted "how dare you look into people's houses, what impudence". It must have taken a great effort to brush aside her shyness that morning.

The red deer used to desecrate the few swedes that were grown on the croft for cattle feed and my dad built a turf hut to hide out with slots to look through and lie in wait for the marauding deer to appear.

One night he went out with a rifle an old army 303 which was lent to him by the gamekeeper with the Baroness's consent. He returned home that night he had shot three hinds, so he had to harness the mare and get the sledge out to take the beasts home over the moor. It was a dangerous operation as there were gulley's and peat bogs littered all over the moor and sometimes, he would have to stop if the clouds hid the moon from view. Nan had passed word round all the neighbours (she was much braver than me) to Johnny next door and Maggie and Lexie for my dad was going to give them all a haunch of venison. It was a bright moonlit night and first on the scene was Maggie with a great big enamel basin. The lure of venison was obviously greater than the fear of being out at night on the Blackfold road.

"Alick" she said "I just want the liver" to which my dad replied "look Maggie you can have any part of the beast you want rump, ribs, sirloin but I can't give you the liver". That was obviously dad's luxury Maggie stamped her feet, hit the basin against the wall and said to dad "you can keep your venison, i don't want any" and with that she shuffled out the door and vanished into the night. I wonder what Lexy and Nellie said when Maggie came home empty handed.

They were a very spirited lot of sisters, as I said before they just blended into the scenery. The tall pine trees swaying around their cabin, the broom, the heather, the bog myrtle all lent themselves to the sisters, they weren't made for Blackfold. Blackfold was made for them. My dad had not long bought a bike for Nan (not much chance of me getting one) I had to wait till my poor granduncle died and I fell heir to his great big work bike, it was a Hercules. By name and build. Lexy must have noticed Nan riding her bike and one day she came to the door and asked my mum if she could borrow the bike to go to the post office at Abriachan a good few miles hence. Lexy was very cripple in one leg and she also had a crooked arm, she walked with a bad limp and her right hand was always on her hip.

My mum was very concerned that Lexy would hurt herself, she said "yes Lexy you can have the bike but are you sure you can still ride a bike it's been a long time since you were last on one'. Lexy retorted, trying to hide her anger "of course I can ride a bike, do you think I'm an invalid or something" Mum said "it's not that Lexy but what will happen if you fall and hurt yourself" I'll be alright Lexy kept saying and eventually mum gave in and gave her the bike. Lexy always wore a green beret and I remember her vanishing round the end of the house pushing the bike out of sight. She would not try to get on it whilst we were watching about ten minutes later who came back round the end of the house but Lexy with a big tuft of grass stuck on her beret and a wet backside. "you can keep your bike" she said it was grudged anyway and she threw it down with some force at my mum's feet. I don't know, but what I think happened was, she had tried to get on the bike and with her bad leg and crooked back she must have fallen off then realised that her cycling days were well behind her. We watched poor Lexy disappear over the horizon on her way to the post office. This reminds me of a story about Lexy that Jimmy Ross the gamekeeper told my dad. In her younger days Lexy had a bike and the woodmen were cutting timber at the foot of the very, very steep Blackfold brae all of a sudden, they heard this whoosh accompanied by a woman's shrill piercing screams. Her brake lever had broken and she came down the big brae at about sixty miles an hour, it was near the Dunain straight before she managed to slow down, she told us later the straight was about a mile and a half along the road.

As I said before Maggie and Lexy had quite a lot of cattle but they had not got a bull. The nearest bull was two or three miles away at Ladycairn farm owned by a lovely gentleman Tommy Fraser although he was known by one and all as Tommy Ladycairn. When one of the cows was in season, sometimes they would be unsure and once Lexy said "that big beast there is in season" Maggie quipped up without thinking "owh shutup yourself is in season". Owh dear

If the cow wasn't properly in season, it meant a return journey to the bull four weeks or so later and believe me once was enough.

When a cow was in season Lexy would come along as nice as ninepence, the old bike episode, the venison liver all swept into the past. Lexy would say would you mind taking one of my cows to Ladycairn. Oh how, oh how, oh how I dreaded that. Some of her cows especially the heifers were very wild, they had never been on a rope or halters in their lives. Even the hardened cowboys of the old wild west would have had a job tethering them

However, my mum and I would have to go along, two of the best hustlers in the Highlands and I was only around nine or ten years old. Our only hope of getting a rope round the cow was to herd a few of them into the byre and that's what we did.

Dad would get a loose rope around the cow's neck and then the final halter for a wee bit more control. Then there was a big shout to open the door and stand clear and then like a wild steer at a rodeo show this cow would appear dragging my dad along. Next minute the beast would stop and refuse to budge, mum and I had to come along with sticks to try and keep the cow moving then just as quick as she stopped, she would take off again dragging whoever was on the end of the halter after her.

I don't know how or why my father never said no to Lexy it was an awful and really dangerous ordeal. Fraught with kicks and butts and pulling you through bushes, nettles etc. However, we always made it and after the bull had serviced the cow, she was usually a lot quieter. so, this was the chance for my dad to have a fag, a Capstan. He would then say to me you hold onto the rope now loon, she's a lot quieter and I'll have a smoke.

Sometime when I would be on the halter, the cow would take off and once she got up speed no one on earth could have stopped her, although I was expected to. The time I remember vividly on the way back to Lexy's the cow took off picking up speed and my legs couldn't run any faster, I lost my balance and found myself been dragged along the road. I was too frightened to let go, my knees and arms were all skinned and I could hear my dad shouting, hang on loon, hang on, don't let her go or she'll end up in inverness. Eventually he could see I was hurt and I couldn't stop the beast anyway and dad shouted. Och just let her go, but why did you not hold onto her in the first place, that was a knack I learned not much later on, you could bring a cow to its knees before it picked up speed.

I don't know how we did it but we always got there, but the only one that got pleasure out of it was the bull I suppose.

I don't know how Maggie came to terms with the male and female mating habits I think she used to look on them as dirty. One day I remember Maggie putting a clocken hen into a canvas sack. tying it with a piece of string and putting the hen in the deepest pool in the burn and pushing it under with the switch she always carried, She kept saying to the hen, Ah you dirty brute, you filthy brute, then a wee screed of Gaelic. I thought she was trying to drown the hen but I learnt later she was trying to get the hen off the clock by dipping her in the cold water. I don't know how she expected chickens.

Maggie and Lexy were always falling out, they had their own cattle, their own hens and Maggie was great for her ducks. Lexy had no time for ducks, dirty brutes she called them. She said when she was young, she cracked open a duck's egg and there was a frog's leg inside it. That put me off duck eggs for life, I have never tasted one. Having their own cows and hens led to heated arguments about whose calf this was whose hens were these and if they found a nest of eggs oh boy that was something else.

They also owned a nice stone-built house called Alickans after their uncle Alick who used to live there, but they stayed well clear of it as Maggie said it was haunted. Alickans house was just about three hundred yards from their cabin a much superior abode than the one the sisters lived in, but as I said it was haunted by a green lady and nobody ventured near it, even the animals gave it wide berth.

Then one-night Maggie had another big bust up with Lexy, they must have had some quarrels, and early in the morning at the crack of dawn Maggie came knocking at our door. Mum took her in and made her a hot cup of tea. She could see Maggie was pale and shaking, clearly upset and out of sorts. Maggie explained that once again she had fallen out with Lexy. I take it that by now you realise just how difficult a character she was to get on with.

Mum said to Maggie, why don't you move along to Alickans old house and do it up a wee bit. Maggie froze on the spot her face turned deathly pale. Oh, Jessie she stammered, that's where I went last night and never again will I set foot in that place. She went on about this green lady and the devil appearing. I was sitting listening to all this and I was as scared as Maggie was. Maggie stayed with us for a couple of days and went home as she cooled off. You can still see the ruin of Alickans just beside the Blackfold road. My Daughter Laura and I went there recently and she took three pictures of the ruin, but when she went to view them on her camera, there was no house there. Now that is strange said Laura. I managed to get a picture with my own camera but I ventured a wee bit closer.

Another story I heard round the fire when i was but a lad was told by my father.

One old frosty night in mid-winter a local crofter went out with his gun to see if he could bag a hare or rabbit, maybe a deer for the pot. There was a crisp covering of snow on the ground and the moon was very bright that night. He crept through the moorland trying to make as little noise as he could, when suddenly he startled a hare which was hiding in a nearby bush, as the hare sped off, he raised his gun took quick aim and fired. The hare bowled over but picked himself up and managed to run in the direction of the croft houses. The crofter knew he had hit the hare as he could see a trail of blood droplets in the moonlit snow. He followed the trail till he came to a house where an old woman lived on her own everyone kept away from her door as it was generally believed that the woman was a witch. The trail of blood led to her back door and from there he could see a glimmer of light at the window. He furtively crept to the window and through a small gap in the curtains, he could see the old women sitting by the fireside with her foot in a basin of water nursing a wound on her leg. Legend has it that a witch could turn herself into a hare whenever she wanted. Well after all this is Blackfold we're talking about and that is the story exactly as I heard it.

It's a very notorious place for ghost and strange happenings is Blackfold. I have spoken to many grown men and none of them would venture up there in the dark. I remember Maggie talking about a certain woman, I don't know who she was, but I suspect she was a bit of a witch and she dabbled in the occult. One night a knock came to her door. She went to answer the door with her little paraffin light and there in the glow standing on the doorstep was this sinister looking figure all dressed in black, she looked down and she had no shoes on just cloven hooves. The woman slammed the door shut and almost fainted with terror. As far as I can remember that woman changed her ways it was a stark warning to her not to interfere with the occult.

My mum often told me this story one evening at Blackfold, she was working out in the garden, it was just early twilight and she was on her knees. Suddenly she felt a cold shiver come over her and she felt as if there was a presence there. She turned slowly around and here was this person standing behind her. She said it was Uncle john Blackfold for whom she came home from London to nurse right through to his death a few years earlier. Oh, James she said his eyes were shining bright just like stars and he was all dressed in white. He asked her for a drink of water. My mother was rooted to the spot and she warned me, if they ever appear like that don't speak to them and especially don't give them anything. Don't ask me why I don't know the reason. Maybe reading "The witch of endor" from the Holy bible might throw some light on it. Then mum said she watched him float away, way over the hills in the direction of the old churchyard at Bona, where most of our kin are buried. I think by now you must know what effect all this was having on me just a seven or eight-year-old boy, but I often used to get mum to recall this event I was so enthralled by it all.

Another strange and frightening event which I will never forget, how could I ever forget, happened many moons ago when I was about eight or nine. This is etched in my mind, yes way back in the dark corridors of my mind and sometimes at night these memories spring from the past right to the front of my mind.

It was the day of the Halloween party which was an annual event held in Dochgarroch Hall just a few hundred yards from the school. It was a crisp moonlit night and there was much excitement in the air as miss McFadyen our teacher led all the children down to the hall. I always remember Baroness Burton's chauffeur Kenny Macgregor was the door keeper a very kindly gentleman and he made everyone welcome with a handshake and a big smile. A lot of the parents came for most of them lived on the lower grounds, but my parents did not come they stayed at home at Blackfold.

There was the usual fun and games dooking for apples, games, tea and cake, something I didn't know much about only that they tasted good. All this was supervised by Mary our teacher to ensure fair play at all times. Our teacher Mary MacFayden was a very firm and strict women, but also a very good living, kindhearted soul. Taught me a lot about how to get through life and I still quote many of her teachings to this day. The world could do with many more Mary McFadyen's. Funny how life pans out, but I remember Mrs McFadyen's nieces playing around the schoolhouse when they stayed with their aunt and just quite recently, I got to know Mary now Sciascia through Facebook. We often exchange a few yarns.

However back to the story as I am starting to wander a wee bit. I remember Nan my sister was off school with the mumps so I was at the party on my own, as of then we had no children for next door neighbours.

As time wore on, I don't know to this day what I was thinking but I thought it was time for me to be going home. Blackfold was almost three miles away all uphill, through tall dark forest a huge deep rocky ravine to the left and of course an old battlefield further up on the right a lot of ingredients for a terrifying walk for a wee boy.

So, off I set as I rather gingerly walked out of the lovely warm hall, out of the bright lights and into the pale shadowy moonlight. To say that I was frightened was an understatement. I was absolutely terrified all those ghost stories that Maggie and Lexy had told kept churning round and round in my head. The narrow path meandered for the first part mainly through thick dark forest. Giant Douglas fir, spruce and wellingtonias creaking and groaning in the wind as if they were asking me what a little boy like me was doing out all alone on a Halloween night.

There are some of the tallest trees in the UK in that part of the forest. I could and I still can remember every twist and turn of that path as I had trod it so many times on my way to school, but I'd never trod it on a dark, albeit a moonlit night. I broke into a run now and again, but that made me worse, my mind kept asking me "what are you running for" you only run when you think someone or worse still something is chasing you, so I slowed down and tried to act calm. Up ahead of me out of the forest there was a deep deep gorge well over 100ft in places, this was carved out or worn out over thousands of years by the waters which I could now hear lapping against the rock's way down below. My dad was never done warning me to never ever go near the edge when going to school as the path we took followed along the edge of the gorge. During the war Canadian Lumberjacks had bulldozed a road along the edge so that they could extract the timber. They are still called the Canadian roads.

Further up the gorge about halfway up there is a waterfall and my dad told me that a little boy had gone too near the edge fell over and put his brains out on one of the jagged rocks. The neighbours marked the spot with a round boulder.

Just up ahead was the battlefield it is marked on the ordinance survey maps. Where just before Culloden two clans settled a dispute over some land. I was told who the two clans were, but I have completely forgotten. Maggie and Lexy had told some strange goings on around this area, the" bad bit" as Lexy used to call it, for when Maggie and Lexy would be walking home up this road, Lexy would say "sheesh, sheesh we're coming to the bad bit now" Maggie would snap back and say "shut up and hold your tongue, we all know about this bad bit". I started getting more afraid than ever as I was fast approaching this bad bit, there was a game keepers house just at the edge of the battlefield where a kindly old lady who was known as granny Ross lived there with her husband, their son Jimmy who had been a game keeper all his life on the estate told us a tale about this house. Mostly at night they would hear footsteps and thumping noises coming from the fireplace. It was so bad, they weren't getting proper sleep, they decided to consult a minister for advice to see what he thought.

There was a big flat hearth stone in front of the fire and this was lifted, they dug down a bit and they found a skeleton of a man most likely killed in the battle. The skeleton was taken away and given a proper burial to I don't know where. Jimmy told us that was the end of the noises, they were never heard anymore. It's a very strange world we live in.

Just as I was approaching the top of the brae where the "bad bit" was and the old cottage. There was this unearthly screech and skirling like a banshee from a giant granny fir tree, I was showered with bits of twig and fur cones. I froze to the spot and started crying. I've seldom if ever been more afraid in my life. I told everyone later it must have been an owl which I startled. But later on I got myself to thinking it might not have been an owl, it was quite dark and I couldn't see very well and in any case owls don't disturb very easily and surely it would have been used to us passing it every day, I'll leave this up to your imagination but I do know I was so scared I could have ran back to the hall but I decided to press on and try to get home, I had passed the bad bit, but it had taken an awful toll on my nerves my heart was thumping and I was crying. Just up ahead there was a fork in the road. The right fork went up a very steep track which ran through tall broom bushes I saw a light, I wiped the tears from my eyes to make sure I wasn't seeing things, but no, sure enough here was this light flickering and heading down the path towards me. All I could think of now was this must be my mum and dad coming to meet me with the paraffin tilly lamp. I started running towards the light by now I was quite hysterical I was almost overcome with emotion, relief, and happiness. I started to whimper "mummy oh mummy".

I kept running stumbling towards the light, ah my dear mummy and safety a warm hand to cling to and take me home, then just as suddenly as it appeared it suddenly disappeared. I don't know where and I don't suppose I ever will but I now have come to believe that God sent a guiding light from above taking me away from the gorge which ran alongside the left fork

By now I was more frightened than ever as I passed by where I thought the light was, I was fully expecting one of Lexy's ghosts to jump out on me. Oh boy was I scared. I often think how I would have coped if I were a grown man, I just don't know.

I furtively made my way up the deer track. I had passed the bad bit but I didn't feel any better, I was probably more frightened than ever. I sometimes wonder how much fear a mind can stand before it has had enough and shut down. I must have been pretty near that limit.

Having past Lexy's bad bit there was something else up ahead of me that I was most scared of something that would surely have made me take the left road to the gorge.

Here we go again, Maggie, Lexy (will they ever go away) told us at one of their ceilidh's about an incident that happened just after the battle of Culloden, two redcoat troopers were rounding up all the wounded and rebel clansman that had fought at the battle and they were ambushed by a bunch of the wild BlackFolders and murdered. They buried them in an old quarry right beside the road that I had to pass to reach home.

Lexy told us that you could hear the trooper's bugles sounding just after midnight, I crept past the quarry and now I had only about a mile to go. First lights I saw were Maggie and Lexy's shining out the split in the curtains and peeping out through the cracks in the wooden wall. I passed Alickans old, haunted house passed Johnny next door and then home sweet home. My mum and dad never locked their door so I just walked in. They were sitting in front of a roaring fire. Dad just said "where on earth have you been and how did you get home" and I think that is all that was said.

When I went back to school on the following Monday Miss McFadyen said" where on earth did you go on Friday, we were all looking for you, I was going to arrange a taxi for you". Oh boy imagine telling me now I thought. If that taxi had come for me, I wouldn't be writing this story.

That very same now Andy my old pal was at the same party, the atmosphere in the hall was very smoky and Andy was a bit asthmatic, so he decided to go out for a breath of fresh air, he started walking towards the canal locks which were only about a hundred yards from the hall. He started walking towards the edge of the locks and was just about to take the last step to the edge when he heard a woman's voice call his name, he turned around but there was no one there. When he looked round again, he discovered that the last step was not a step at all but the moons reflection on the water. Had it not been for the voice he would have taken what surely would have been his last step and ended up in the canal. Nobody who fell into the locks got out. It has claimed many lives. One of which I will now tell is as sad a story as you will ever hear.

My old pal Donald John was lock keeper there for many years and his house was directly in front of the locks, only a stone throws away. Donald was in the tower as they call it where all the controls are, it was mid-winter and 2" of snow lay on the ground. They had a wee toddler just over two and a half years old and Donald's wife was just making the supper. She told her wee mannie to go to the garden gate wave the torch and daddy would come in for his supper. Donald came in a wee while after and just as he sat down, he said "where is the wee man" oh said Betty "I thought he was with you" oh dear me said Donald and he rushed outside only to find someone had left the garden gate open. He followed the wee footprints to the edge of the canal and then they disappeared. The wee man had gone right over the edge and into the water. The poor wee soul didn't make it, what with the ice-cold water and drop of some twelve feet he didn't survive. Poor Donald and his wife what more can I say.

In 1955 we had the worst snowstorm in living memory, the drifts were right over the house tops and the corn stacks. Cattle were starving and people were right out of supplies. Nothing could get through. Maggie and Lexy ploughed their way through the snow up and over the drifts and sometimes disappearing if there was a burn or a soft spot below, to reach our croft and ask my dad for some fodder for her cattle. My dad was very firm with her he said "I told you Lexy to stock up, this storm was forecast you should have ordered a load of hay last week". My dad did give her as much sheaves as she could carry, having knocked most of the oats off first with an old-fashioned flail. Nan and I also went along dodging the drifts with as much as we could carry, the ground was bare in places where the wind had blown it all away against walls and hollows, so you could navigate a course no matter how twisted. The army had to step in that year and they dropped bales of hay and provisions by helicopter thus they called it "operation snowdrop". The next few paragraphs should actually appear a little later on, but it gives a wee description of the Shaws on my mother's side, so I've decided to leave it just as it is

There were also other members of the Shaw family old granny Shaw had fourteen of a family all brought up in the wee but and ben at lower Dunain. It's hard to imagine where they all slept and how they all managed around the dinner table. Uncle Hugh the eldest was a giant of a man 6ft 7inches in his stocking soles and the rest of the family weren't small by any means. On the death of aunty Belle Dunain uncle Hugh being the eldest of the fourteen became heir, but at this time he and his wife Kate were awaiting passage to Australia under a government scheme which set him up with a lovely cabin on the seashore, a good number of acres of land and a jersey cow dairy herd. So, in view in all this it was Uncle Hugh's wish that the croft be left to his niece Jessie Ann, my mother. A letter was passed round the rest of the family stating his wishes and there were no objections, so my mum fell heir to the croft.

On his arrival in Australia, Uncle Hugh sent my dad a letter urging him to come and join him, he wrote "We have a beautiful place here, a lovely house, rolling acres of land sweeping down to the beach and a pedigree jersey cattle herd for dairy produce". Mum and dad swithered over it for a while but decided to stay in Bonnie Scotland. I often wonder how i would have got on had we emigrated. I sure would have hoped that I didn't meet the same fate as my grand uncle Donald, Uncle Hugh's brother who emigrated to New Zealand.

Britain was colonising these commonwealth countries at the time and encouraging people to settle there. Uncle Donald applied for a position with the Royal New Zealand mounted police and in due course he got a favourable reply. Passage paid and all necessary papers provided.

The Shaw's were great people for wandering and so one fine day Uncle Donald bade a last fond farewell to all his kin at Lower Dunain and set sail into the great unknown territories of New Zealand. Uncle Donald arrived safely and by all accounts did very well with his job as a mounted police officer. However, one day there was a robbery and a murder committed in the town where he was stationed and several Maori tribesmen were seen fleeing the scene. Uncle Donald was ordered to go after them on horseback into the bush and bring them back to justice. I don't think that should have been a one-man job, but however Donald obeyed his orders and rode away in pursuit of the Maoris. Next day, late afternoon Uncle Donald's horse came running back to the police station, without his rider. Uncle Donald was never found, people knew the Maori's were a cannibalistic tribe or race and they ate their captives. My mum always said that is what happened to poor Uncle Donald. I don't know what happened after that, if they ever caught the culprits but I would think there would be a record kept somewhere in that police station. In the little church yard at Bona both Johnny Dunain R.A.F and Uncle Donald R.N.Z.M.P are commemorated on the family gravestone, both reported missing presumed dead. You will read about Johnny Dunain just a little later on.

This book is throwing up a lot of questions which I would dearly love answered, but I suppose will never be. If I was younger, I would get to Rheins in France where Johnny Dunain was shot down, then to Arras and Ypres where my grandad was killed and still lying there and maybe then to New Zealand to see what I could find out. Depending on what time I'm allowed I might just do that although it is very doubtful.

(Mum taking peats for the fire in her apron at
Blackfold she carried everything in her apron.
kindlers, eggs peats, tatties etc)

(Uncle Hugh Shaw and wife)

During operation snowdrop in 1955 my granny's sister Belle Dunain died on her croft at Lower Dunain, this left the croft to her brother Uncle Hugh Shaw, but he had no interest in it regarding himself as he and his wife had booked their passage to New Zealand, where a nice little farm holding awaiting them with a jersey herd of dairy cattle, part of a government scheme at the time.

It was Uncle Hugh's wish that his niece, my mum should be left the croft and a letter went round the rest of the family without objection. In these days one was not allowed to hold two crofts at the same time, so they decided to give up the croft at wester Blackfold.

So the big day came when my folks decided to move down to Lower Dunain and civilisation, my folks were really poor, dad couldn't afford a cattle float all the livestock would have to walk down to Dunain, a task that would be nigh impossible nowadays. Dad was very secretive almost shy to a point, he waited until twilight when he knew there would be little to no traffic on the road and we set off. There were five cows plus three calves, our calves and cows were a lot quieter than Lexy's the cows were all used to being tethered and we had a cow called Rosy who was a sort of matriarch on a halter led by my dad and the rest of the stock followed, the calves were a bit of a problem as they kept wandering side to side and Nan and I had to run after them and get them back in line. Nan also had two nanny goats on tethers a few pet lambs which followed my mum everywhere, so they were ok. We also had about a dozen hens tied in canvas sacks and strapped onto Sally the horse and of course all the cats, they were Nan and I's pets. There was also Glen the big rough collie dog he kept the lambs in order as well. The cats were Nan and I's big concern, they were our pets after all, my main cat was Tiger. Nan was very jealous of this cat as she used to hammer most of her cats. She used to say "Tiger is my cat" and she would grab her of my lap where she usually sat and put her on her knee. As soon as I called Tiger she would always come back to me, Tiger was just like a guard dog she would follow me everywhere and I suppose that's how all the cats made it to Lower Dunain, they all followed Tiger. My dad said she was the result of one of our cats Topsy mating with a wild cat. Now and again, you would hear a screech and a curse as dad kept tripping over the cats. Then dad would say "we should have left those blinking cats at home". I didn't expect any of us thought the cats would have followed us, we would have just gone back for them the next day.

Going back to Tiger I was sitting by the fire one night as she climbed up and lay on my lap. She was old by then and dad said "that cat is going to die". Tiger knew she was going to die and it was her last act of sheer faithfulness to me as she curled up and went to sleep so nice warm and cosy and she never woke up, that was one of the saddest days of my life. I could write a whole book about her, but maybe later on I might tell you about some of her exploits. She is buried along with all the other cats and dogs in the garden of the old croft at Lower Dunain.

For the life of me I don't know how we ever made it to Lower Dunain especially in the dark but we did. We managed to lock the animals in the only fenced field on the croft. When the dawn broke on aunty Belles's croft we awoke after a short sleep and everything and everyone was there, Billy Smarts circus had arrived, cows, calves' horse, nanny goats which Nan had tied up pet lambs bleating at the gate waiting for their bottle.

Glenn our collie dog and oh yes, all the cats were there good old Tiger was on my knee once again.

Just like Blackfold the croft house at Lower Dunain had no electric, no running water, no toilet but it had one great luxury Aunty Belle had left a tabletop calor gas cooker with two burners, what a boon for my poor mum, although my mum used to still cook on the open fire when the gas cylinder was empty.

My dad was still working on the estate dragging wood with the horse and mum did most of the work on the croft. When the cows were outside in the summer, much rather than herding them all up to the byre for milking she used to lasso them and wait till they dragged her near a tree and she would wrap the end of a rope around it and secure the cows. Then she would fetch her pail and wee three-legged stool and milk the cow. This was very time consuming and extremely sore on the wrists till one got used to it. Then the calves had to be pail fed, that was my father's way of doing things, of course that means we had a steady supply of milk for the table, otherwise the calves would suck the cows dry.

In the winter the cattle were kept in and just let out for water for maybe an hour or so. This would give me a chance to muck the byre out without the fear of getting kicked.

One of the biggest laughs I ever had on the croft and indeed maybe ever involved our cats. I'll never forget my mum was going to milk the cows there were four of them in this part of the byre two double stalls side by side. The cats knew it was milking time they would hear the rattle of the milk pail and they would sit in a straight-line right behind cows on the other side of the drain channels. Mum used to squirt the milk out of the cow's teats just like a water pistol and aim it at the cat's mouths. The cats loved this and they would lick the milk off their faces with their paws.

When cows are fed rich food such as swedes they can become very loose in their bowel movements, this cow she was called Heather was chewing on a swede when a piece stuck in her throat, she gave a mighty cough to try and dislodge it and a big skoosh of coo sharn came splashing out with some force, the cats about ten of them were covered from head to toe even the lower part of the byre door got splattered. You know how cats like to keep themselves clean, they were trying to tiptoe through the sharn but there was hardly a square inch that wasn't covered. The cats were trying to clean themselves licking their paws and then shaking their heads at the horrible taste. A few licks and a few rubs and they were jumping about all over the place. The coos sharn was stuck on that byre for many years, the sun had baked it dry. Next day the cats were back in the byre but they were spread out more and sitting way further back in the balcony so to speak.

Probably the sweetest voice I ever heard in my life was my mother's, she was always singing, I suppose it took some of the drudgery out of her work. She always sang to the cows when she was milking. On warm summer evenings you would hear her sweet voice drifting out the byre door travelling as if it were on some magic carpet. She always said the cows liked her singing it relaxed them and they would let their milk down more readily. This was proved many years later, in large modern milking parlours the farmers piped in music played on speakers throughout the parlour. The cows produced much more milk or at least didn't hold any. Mum had quite a large repertoire of songs. "Ca the ewes tae the knowes" was her real favourite. "The rose of Tralee" I could have listened to her all night "the wild mountain thyme" "gentle maiden amongst many others, I wish I had a tape recorder back then.

There were always great commotions at hay time, it was usually a race against the weather. Dad cut all the hay four or five acres with the scythe which had to be like a razor, he would sharpen it down on one knee every forty yards or so. The scythe left the grass in neat swathes, which was turned over several times until it was almost dry but not too dry as most of the goodness would evaporate out of it.

Then we had to put it into small rucks about six feet high and they had to be waterproof. There was a special art in this, when nearing the top, I used to tease the top into the shape of a bonnet and then place it on top of the ruck. Dad used to say to my poor mum "Why can't you make your rucks like the loon; all his ones are bone dry". They were okay if it didn't rain but if it did rain the water could soak a couple of feet down into the ruck. When the ruck was finished, we used to tease and twist grass ropes out of the ruck to keep the wind from blowing the top off. Dad never told me about my waterproof rucks I never got credit for anything, not that I expected it, it was just a way of life it had to be done. I often wonder who showed me how to build waterproof hay rucks. The same person that taught the birds to make their nest's I suppose.

When the hay had seasoned in the rucks and it was thought safe to put them into bigger stacks, that was another job I was quite afraid of as I had to build the stack. When it got near the top dad would put me up on a ladder to finish it, with these words "your much slamper than me boy, you can finish it off". The stacks could be twelve maybe fifteen feet high and they got very shaky the further you went up, you had to stand in the middle of the stack where it was more stable then you would hear a shout from below "where are you loon? Put a wee bit more on the west side it's awful bare looking". Then the whole stack would shoggle from side to side as I tried to keep my balance. As dad forked up the last bundle of hay, I would hear those welcoming words "That'll do now loon you can come down, I'll get the ladder". The ladder I'll always remember was a homemade one, my dad was very knacky. Only problem was he was the only one strong enough to lift it. Then the final bit, stack rope was slung over the stack at several intervals and heavy stones tied to the ends to keep a constant pressure on the stack which would sink to about eight foot in height. I heard of hay stacks, really big ones going on fire if the hay was not properly cured internal combustion, they call it, but that never happened to us.

At harvest time all the corn was cut by the scythe, that was before dad got a tractor. Mum and I had to gather the corn into sheaves, make straw bands by twisting several strands of straw together and tie the sheaves. I hated that job, apart from the sore back the straw was often mixed with thistle and dead nettle and I don't need to tell you how sharp they are, of course all I got was "don't be such a pansy boy, you're not afraid of a few thistles are you". It was ok for dad to say that, he had hands like steel he could crush a handful of hazelnuts with his bare hands.

Mum spent most of the day out in the fields in all weathers (I don't think oilskins were around then) milking, hoeing, turnips fencing, cutting sticks for the fire carting turnips home on her back. Andy would tell you all about that.

Occasionally mum would go to town, usually to pay some bills that were long overdue. On the croft she dressed like a tramp half a dozen old jerseys thrown on. Sleeves of old jerseys she wore for stockings. Bag apron tied with stackrope or baler twine and any old shoes or boots that would fit. Poor mum my dear mum, she used to laugh and say "The scarecrow you made is better dressed than me". She always had a sense of humour even through all her trials and setbacks. But when mum went to town you would not know Her. Lovely costume, blouse, butterfly broach, pearl necklace and a gorgeous wide brimmed hat, sometimes with a small feather attached. Her time in Pitmain Lodge and down in London working for the gentry was obvious when you looked at her. Andy's dad Ian Kennedy once told me one Tuesday at the cattle mart he banged into my mum and he said "you know Jimmy I met a lot of woman in town today, but the best looking one I saw was your mum" you see I never saw her dressed like that before and Andy's dad wasn't akin to throwing compliments about, Mum had beautiful clothes in her wardrobe she had taken back from London and she said "there's clothes in here I will never wear" and a good lot of them she never did, poor mum.

One day I was coming home from town I was probably out on the bash the night before and I met my mum halfway up on the croft road on her way to catch the bus. Poor mum she was pretty frustrated and more than a little annoyed at me coming at that time of day she said "Jimuck (she quite often called me that) I'll never get to town today I'm going to miss the bus for following her was an entourage of animals. The animals knew that mostly when they saw mum it meant they were going to get fed. Her three pet lambs, about two dozen hens including Jockey the rooster and a host of cats. As I said mum was the one who usually fed them and they followed her everywhere, they were no strangers to me either and they all knew my voice and I managed to distract them and drive them home, and my mum made her escape as I watched her disappear around the corner.

(John Shaw in Uniform and full rear gunner uniform)

(John Shaw, my uncle Johnny Dunain at his
marriage to Lily Marello not long after the last
tragic mission, my mum is bridesmaid)

Sergeant

John Mcdonald Shaw

1050043, 405 Sqdn., Royal Air Force Volunteer Reserve who died on 29 June 1944 Age 34

Son of Isabella Shaw, of Dunain, Inverness-shire; husband of Elizabeth Shaw, of Dunain.

Remembered with Honour
Runnymede Memorial

Commemorated in perpetuity by
the Commonwealth War Graves Commission

As I stated earlier my granny's sister Belle who lived on the croft at Lower Dunain died in 1955 she was known to all and Sundry as Belle Dunain and a very kind and affectionate women she was. She loved her ceilidh's and could rattle a tune or two out of an old melodeon she had, she gave it to me as it was falling apart, the cardboard bellows was full of holes and it was kept together by tape and sticking plasters. Aunty Belle lived with her brother Calum and her son Johnny who was also always called Johnny Dunain.

Just before the outbreak of World War two.

Johnny married his childhood sweetheart Lilly Marello and they lived not too far away at upper Dunain, but here alas a tragic story unfolds.

Johnny joined up with the RAF bomber command and his position was rear gunner with the Lancaster heavy bombers. My mother recalled the time Johnny came home on leave to visit his wife and he then popped down to the croft to say hello to his mum, aunty Belle. He stayed a while and when it was time to go he bade his dear mum and my mum a very fond farewell. He disappeared around the corner and then came into view again as he walked up the steep brae which led down to the croft, as he reached the top of the brae he stopped and turned around to take a last long look at the wee housey that he was brought up in and he could see us waving goodbye. He was just a blur to us as we saw him disappear through tear-stained eyes. Aunty Belle turned to mum with tear filled eyes and said "ahh, Jessie I just get the feeling that's the last we'll see of Johnny".

Uncle John was sgt rear air gunner R.A.F.V.R

(pathfinder force who flew on board the Lancaster heavy bombers which were involved in the Dambuster raid over Germany. One night in June 1944 the Lancaster bomber took off from Grandsden lodge at 23:05 to bomb railyards in France in support of the invasion at Dunkirk. They were attacked at 12.000ft by a lone Nazi night fighter the plane was badly hit and burst into flames. There were five other crew on board, including a Canadian pilot F.A Smitten who shouted to Johnny "get out quick we're on fire and going down quick" Uncle Johnny never made it out as far as we knew nor did the other gunner F/SGT G.W Moore.

The Pilot P/O Smitten Nav sgt E.E Thornton, H Eng., F/O L.R Stein survived and evaded capture. Bomb aimer P/O E.W Stringham captured and taken P.O.W the Nazi M.E 109 fighters always attacked from the rear and with Uncle Johnny being a rear Gunner he would have been the first target. So, Johnny never returned. On his gravestone these few words read. Reported missing presumed killed in action.

Just after the war the Canadian pilot visited Johnny's mother, Aunty Belle on the croft at Lower Dunain and told her he thought he saw Johnny jump from the wreck on its way down, but he was never found, unless he was captured and died in captivity or buried by some of the local French farmers. His widow Lilly saw a fortune teller who told her that Johnny would return home to her and every day for I don't know how many years poor Lilly waited for that shadow to pass her window, that knock on the door. The oh so familiar voice "I'm home darling" which never came. Jonny was 34 when he died, so, if Johnny had not been killed, he probably would have fallen heir to the croft, we'll never know.

Mrs. Mary McFadyen was our primary teacher in Dochgarroch a school tucked away in a wooded countryside area. The school had the highest 11+ pass rate of any school in the country. She was a wonderful teacher very firm; you did what you were told or else. Could do with a few Miss MacFayden's today. You were taught to respect your parents and elders. Respect life, person and property plus a great religious belief in God and our Lord Jesus Christ. I for which I am in this troubled world so very grateful. She taught all manners of things her repertoire knew no bounds and bear in mind she taught five classes simultaneously, apart from the standards maths, English, geography, history etc. She taught in crafts and art, gym, music, Gaelic, gardening for the boys, sewing and knitting for the girls, not least was her first aid skills a talent she was very often called when to put onto practice.

Miss MacFayden was very practical and thrifty, you had to be in those days and also very tidy. Throwing litter away was a punishable offence by getting two or three wraps on the hand with her two-pronged strap, a most feared article, but if you got it or pandys as my dad used to call it, you deserved it. We had rubbers or erasers and pencils then biros were never used if we wrote essays, they were done old styles pen and ink. The inkwells were stuck into our desks and we each took turns to fill them with this horrible black school ink. What a mess was made sometimes, of course we had blotters then to soak away surplus ink that had been spilt.

If we had to rub something out and she spotted you she would stop you in your tracks and ask "what are you rubbing out now'. She would like to see the mistake first. Too much rubbing out caused quite a kerfuffle.

To save paper we used to do a lot of work on slates especially spelling and sums, where it was much easier to rub out a wet finger usually did the trick. The pupils who could afford then bought lovely wooden framed slates, but for people like Andy and I, Jim Paterson was another used ordinary roofing slates you had to be very careful you didn't drop them or they would break your toes if they landed on your feet.

I was still at Dochgarroch school at the time we moved from Blackfold to Lower Dunain. So I no longer had to walk two and half miles each way it was now reduced to the one mile. This reminds me of a few incidents that happened about that time. Andy my old pal who lived on a farm just about a mile away from the croft as the crow flies was playing at soldiers with the rest of the children. He had found an old pan discarded in the nearby rubbish dump, the ones with the round handles, like pails. He stuck it on his head, this was ok he just looked the part Sir Lancelot himself would be proud of such head gear but then he gave the handle a mighty pull and it slid under his chin just like a guardsman's helmet. Now I can run said Andy, there's no fear of it falling off now, oh boy how right he was. Just then our teacher Miss MacFadyen shouted "come along children, come along playtimes over" We all scurried into the school. Miss MacFadyen took a look around her classes and noticed Andy was missing, sort of absent without leave "where's Andrew?" she asked. Moira one of the pupils said "please miss, he's still over the wall with a pan stuck on his head "silly boy she said you'd better come with me" Poor teacher she was always climbing over that wall. There were three horseshoe steps like a sort of stile built into the wall.

We all rushed out and here's Andy with this rusty old pan firmly stuck on his head, he was trying to find the steps but he kept banging into the outside toilet wall and one of the big oak trees. All we could hear was Andy moaning help, "please help me I can't see". For us the toy battle was over but for Andy it was just beginning. Miss MacFadyen told Moira the head pupil to go the stick shed where she had an assortment of old rusty world war one tools. Moira came back with a screwdriver and old rusty hacksaw and oh no for petes sake no a blacksmiths hammer.

Moira handed the screwdriver to Miss MacFadyen just like a surgeon's nurse at the operating table. Miss MacFadyen grabbed Andy by the pan handle. She tried to straighten the big lug that kept the handle onto the pan. "Keep still will you" she kept saying and with that she gave the screwdriver a sharp twist and it slipped giving Andy a big graze on his unprotected chin. Sorry Andrew she said but if you'd kept still that would not have happened. I don't know what Andy was saying, it was just a series of moans and ouch that hurts. Next tool was a file but that wasn't having much effect apart from the buzzing in Andy's ears, then she tried the hacksaw. There were sparks flying everywhere and teacher said to us "good, I think we're making some headway at last." Then halfway through the handle the blade broke and all that was left was the hammer, when everything else fails there's always the good old hammer. Miss MacFadyen started banging on the half-cut piece of metal gingerly at first but hitting harder every stroke. Poor miss MacFadyen was getting worried by now and Andy was wondering if he would ever hear again at the punishment his eardrums were taking, every blow was like thunder inside that pan. By this time a good few of the neighbours had come down, they said "we heard the banging and wondered what an earth was going on" when they saw Andy, they all burst out laughing Mrs. Main laughed the loudest, she said "that's the old pan I threw out a couple of weeks ago" now with people to cheer her on Mis MacFadyen gave the pan handle one last mighty well aimed blow and that did the trick, the lug that held the handle onto the pan broke and Andy was free as Miss MacFadyen twisted the pan off his head Andy was going round in circles by this time just like a boxer been hit by a knockout punch. Miss MacFadyen told Andy to sit down and Moira went and fetched a glass of nice cool clear water.

"Now" said Miss MacFadyen "let that be a lesson to you and no more objects on your head" and with that she grabbed the pan and with a mighty heave just like a Olympic hammer thrower she hurled the pan as far as she could into the bushes "that's the last you'll see of that she said". But I'm not too sure about that, sometimes when the moon is full if you look up you'll see a strange object orbiting the moon. Well, I don't know about a strange but to Andy it may look quite familiar.

Dochgarroch school could be quite a dangerous school at playtime especially where soldiers, cowboys and Indians were involved. The following incident almost ended my life, I still get shivers thinking about it. This day it was cowboys and Indians we were playing and one of my school pals Dennis Barton was looking for some sort of weapon. We used to make bows out of hazel sticks and arrows out of raspberry canes. They were all pointed, most of us carried pocketknives. Dennis decided to make a spear and he plucked a tall dead shrub out of the ground and whittled a fine point on it. Suddenly without warning he shouted "I'll take your height Jim" and he hurled the spear at just above my head. Something like William Tell, but his aim wasn't as good as Tells. I can't remember if I tried to duck or dodge but I really didn't have time. The spear struck me just a quarter of an inch away from my right eye, it sliced my skin and lodged between my scalp and my skull. All I could feel was this searing pain and the warm blood flowing down my cheek. Of course, all the children climbed over this wall and ran to tell Miss MacFadyen "What on earth is wrong now" she said. Once again Moira was the chief spokesperson "please Miss, James is going about with a spear stuck in his head" What next Miss MacFadyen said as she rushed over to this wall where beyond lay the playing field, she took a look at me, for now I was lying on the ground she got an awful fright she thought I was dead. I can remember the spear had some grip as the shaft was barbed and rough. With a gentle tug she pulled the spear out and told Moira to go and fetch a bottle of iodine and some cotton wool from the medicine chest. Moira soon returned and Miss MacFadyen slapped a big dollop of iodine and that was that. I think I remember her threatening to put a couple of stitches in the wound, but no I was up and about in minuets, no doctor, no tetanus. It was all agreed if that spear had been a quarter an inch further to the right it would have burst my eye and entered my brain (although Miss MacFadyen often told me I hadn't got a brain) and I wouldn't be sitting her writing my story.

I visited the old school lately and they were engrossed by the old tales I told them. They just couldn't believe that we were allowed to take knives to school, but none of us ever dreamt of using them as a weapon against each other.

Miss MacFadyen our teacher was a real character just like my mum you couldn't invent them or the tales that are told about them.

Miss MacFadyen had an old square baby Austin, four which she frequently drove to town, she must have been pretty handy as not many people had a driving licence back then. Some of the old cars had no starter motors you had to crank them from the front with a starting handle. One afternoon she told us she would be letting us out early as she had to go to town on some pressing business. She then turned to Willie Wylie the oldest pupil in the school and a right tearaway to boot, oh Willie, Anne Barton told me that you could drive, you quite often take Bill Pirrie's car for a spin. Willie didn't know what to say he thought he was in for a right thrashing. Someone had clyped on him. Bill Pirrie like most people back then left their cars open and if Bill was away fishing or having a snooze Willie would take the car for a spin and return it and Bill never knew, but he did wonder how his old car was using so much petrol, but to Willies surprise and mine also Miss MacFadyen said "I wonder if you would go out and start my car for me "Willie was only too happy to oblige. The car was garaged, so Willie went around the front got the starting handle but he never checked if it was in gear. It so happened that it was and fortunately it was reverse gear for when he cranked it up it shot out the garage backwards but luckily it stalled, hitting the door post with only a few minor scratches on the rear wing. These things would just not happen nowadays.

(Dochgarroch school pupils with Miss
McFadyen, I'm 2nd from left front row)

Moira Williamson seems to be mentioned a lot in this book she was a really lovely clever girl. Poor Moira died very young she was only in her early twenties and whilst sitting in her armchair by the fire she suddenly said oh mummy I don't ....

And with that she just passed away. Jock Maclean the local grocers van came to the school once a week Miss MacFadyen bought most of her groceries from him, she would allow the children out to the van if they had money, but not many. One of the pupils was a poor orphan girl Anna Macaskill she was a poor soul always getting her sums and her reading wrong. This day she had scraped enough money to buy a bottle of lemonade and she was allowed out to the van. She asked Jock for a bottle of lemonade and Jock said Yes, took the money and told Anna to take the bottle out of the crate beside the driver's seat. Anna came back into the class sat down and unscrewed the bottle top. She said Oh look at the lovely bubbles on the label on the bottle. She was just about to take a gulp when Moira shouted don't drink that that you silly girl. It was a bottle of Parazone bleach Anna had picked up from the wrong crate. She was obviously attracted to the lovely colorful label. As the years rolled slowly by it was time to say goodbye to Dochgarroch school and start my secondary education at the Technical school, now called Inverness High. Farewell to miss MacFadyen, my best pals Andy and a guy called Jim Patterson of whom you will hear a wee bit more later on. High school was tough back then most teachers were very strict and much too eager to give you the belt, four to six cross handers were the norm. I'm all for the belt for cheek, disrespect, serious bad conduct, bullying etc but when it comes to schoolwork a big definite no some pupils are not so clever as the others. A classic example was a horrible woodwork teacher called Fuzzy. One pupil had not got the faintest clue about woodwork, but he excelled in other subjects. We were making kitchen stools and poor Colin could not get the ends of the legs square, He kept whittling the three-foot legs down in an effort to get them square but they were now only about a foot long. Some people have no sense of humour. Fuzzy told all the pupils to gather round his workbench, took out his belt, he called it the persuader, he pointed out Colin's mistakes (Colin Heape was the boy's name) and he said now I'm going to make a heap of Heape on the floor. Then he lashed the belt down with all the venom he could muster. I never felt so sorry for anyone in my life Colin's hands and wrists were terribly marked and he just walked about with both his hands under opposite oxters occasionally taking them out to blow on them, of course poor Colin could not do any more woodwork for the rest of the afternoon. What Fuzzy did that afternoon has lived with me all my life, maybe at long last it will vanish from the depth of my mind into oblivion as I have now taken it out in the open. When I came home from school it was straight into my old work clothes and rags, and right out to the field to work at whatever was going on. School clothes were too precious to be worn working on the croft. My folks just couldn't afford a lot of clothes no designer gear in those days. Woolworths bumper shoes, my cousins cast offs sent from Blackpool and Kent.

I had not much time for homework at night, there was always work to be done when all the other kids were out playing, I had to work. Gordy my next-door neighbour at Lower Dunain, used to come down the brae to my house, with his six-shooter strapped in his belt and a bow and quiver of arrows on his back. I had a fork and a spade on my shoulder.

Threshing the oats of the sheaves was another hard job. the threshing mill was driven by hand, my mum and I used to take turns at winding the big handle it was a two handed job, you had to keep a good steady pace up or you would hear a bawl above the noise of the machine,(a wee bit faster loon). My father did no work on a Sunday so Saturday was a double thresh to take us over the weekend. I never ever thought we could get through it all, there was a mountain of straw when we were finished.

My dad fed the sheaves into the mouth of the mill, a job he thought too dangerous for mum and I. Many a farm worker lost a hand or an arm, being dragged into the big drum which was lined with rows of teeth

Turning the threshing mill was really a gut-wrenching job and I was only eleven getting on twelve at the time. But one sale day a lorry arrived and sitting on the back was a threshing mill, same old handle, but at the back there were two large wooden pedals to assist the handles. There was a tall three-legged stool my dad sat on, fed the sheave into the mill and peddled at the same time. This was a very welcome machine but still very hard work. My sister Nan wasn't much on the scene as she had a job as a domestic at Raigmore hospital, and then Dunain house.

We also had another machine called a fanner. All the oats' bits of straw and chaff were fed into this machine which was driven by a handle just like the threshing machine, but nowhere near as hard to turn. All the rubbish was blown out one end and the nice clean outs fell down a chute into a pail

The chaff was lighter than feathers and my mattress was always stuffed with chaff, every year at fanning time the old chaff was taken out of the bolster mattress and I got a new chaff bed. It was the comfiest bed in the house, mum would occasionally take forty winks on it and say that it really was the comfiest bed in the house.

One day I arrived home from town and I found my mum had been taken into hospital. I always worried about my mum, she had tried to work the fanners on her own and her fingers got caught and crushed between the two big cog wheels, her four fingers were burst open, there was blood all over the barn floor. Her fingers were in some mess the surgeons managed to save mums fingers but they were never the same again

When she came home, she just looked at me and said och Jimuck your meant to get knocks and bumps in this world, it's not meant to be easy, as I grew older, I found this to be true.

By good fortune the milking season was over for she would never have managed to milk the cows but knowing my mum she would have carried on with her good left hand. The cows were afraid of my dad for when he appeared in the doorway, they would all get very restless, they would stamp their feet and swish their tails. My mum used to say to him go away Alick your unsettling them.

Then one day Mr. Stewart the estate clerk of works called, He said to my dad" Alick I never paid you for the work you did with the horse dragging the wood, but I did promise you I would put the water in for you in lieu of payment". This was something special especially for mum. The estate put in a new fireplace with a back boiler to heat the water. They put in a sink with hot and cold taps in the scullery but alas no flush toilet, they also put a standpipe outside for the cattle and that was that.

Next luxury to come to the croft was the electric, that was around 1959. No more candles or paraffin lamps apart from the tilly storm lanterns for outside work.

On the subject of tilly lamps there was always work to be done in the big barn. The oats had to be cleaned for seed and this was always left for night. the big barn was a structure my dad had dismantled at Blackfold and taken down and erected at Dunain. This night I saw my dad filling the tilly lamp and lighting it the electric wasn't in the barn at this time.

I knew I would have to go out to help as I usually did, but I was still eating my supper. Dad wasn't long gone when he came back in, put the lantern on the table and to my surprise he let the air out which extinguished the supply of paraffin. He was visibly shaken and as white as a sheet, Mum said to him "what's wrong Alick you look terrible are you alright?". "Oh, Jesse he said what a fright I got out in the barn tonight. I thought the roof was going to come off, there was someone or something banging on the corrugated iron roof and there wasn't a breath of wind about." This banging went on for a good minute or so. It only stopped when I decided to leave, I'm not going back out there tonight". In fact, it was a good while before he did go back to that barn at night. I never felt at ease in that barn after that, even in the daytime, sometimes I would feel a cold shiver come over me.

Next morning Kenny Chisholm the postman called. He said I hear Lexy died last night. My dad said yes, I knew there was a death somewhere on Blackfold and he told Kenny about the barn.

(Top me outside old croft house door at
Dunain, middle my Granny outside barn next
door, bottom Mum outside croft door)

Now that we were away from Blackfold we thought life would be a bit easier, which I suppose it was, but it was a much bigger place, about twenty five acres, so there were more jobs to do, more livestock, more crops to grow to try make the place a more viable project.

When dad was working away in the woods mum would be out working, lifting stones off the ploughed fields, carting turnips home on her back when the horse was not there.

Sally the horse was getting old now and really not up to the hard work although she would have worked till, she dropped, but dad was so very good to his horses they were very well looked after.

Sally was such a magnificent beast just a model Clydesdale, chestnut brown big white blaze down her face and four white socks. Maclean Barevan a horse dealer said to my dad. "You should get a Foal out of that mare, what a beautiful horse, but dad never did, the horse could not work when heavy in foal and everything had to work, even the cats we were not supposed to feed them or they would not hunt, but we always did. Sally was replaced by a younger mare, we called Polly she was another nice docile horse. The horse was more often at home now dad got more manual work with the forestry. The estate had bought a new Fordson major tractor with a winch for dragging the timber so the horse was very seldom needed.

(Auntie Belle, Auntie Jessie, Uncle Malcolm Dalreoch
lower Dunain, Bottom. Top Uncle Jack cousin
Alan Bamber and dad in the background)

One day I came home from work and I noticed that there was no sign of Polly the horse, I used to give her the heal of the loaf, she loved bread. Sometimes if we were near the house while working mum would go and make a cup of tea, Polly always got a piece at teatime. When mum would shout "Alick the teas ready" Polly would cock her ears up turn her head round and give a neigh in anticipation of her bit of bread.

"So, where's Polly" I asked my mum, "oh dad sold the horse you'd better go around the back of the big barn. I went around the back and sitting there was this wee grey petrol paraffin tractor, freshly painted. Oh boy I didn't know what to think, dad had never driven a tractor in his life, he was brought up with horses on the farms and crofts, so I was rather wary of his driving abilities especially when my mum told me a yarn about it many years ago.

Down on one of the sheds at Blackfold dad had this old motor bike it was partly covered in dust and cobwebs it was an Indian. I remember the big Indian on the fuel tank it also had a rubber trumpet hooter, but we weren't allowed to touch the bike. I said to mum "why doesn't dad use the motor bike down in the shed instead of walking everywhere?" oh she said "when your dad and I were courting he was showing off on the bike and he crashed it into a tree". Mum was on the pillion but there was no damage done as he was crawling, but he never went on the bike again.

He bought the tractor from Tom Macmillan Bogroy and he soon accumulated some of the essential implement's plough, grubber etc. Tom gave him a quick rundown on where the controls were, starter button, clutch, brakes etc. The starter button was never much used as the battery was usually flat and a new one was very expensive. So, we had to rely on the old starting handle and there was a knack in starting these tractors, a knack my dad never quite got the grasp of. If the engine was stopped while running on paraffin it just would not start. It had to be started on petrol by the use of a two-way tap. I used to sneak out at nights drain the remaining dregs of paraffin and make sure there was petrol in the glass bowl to start with, when the engine warmed up you could change it over to paraffin which was much cheaper to run.

Of course, one day, aye and many days it wouldn't start. Dad would be cranking the handle for ages and not cheap. Then the mega temper would take over. When the bonnet came off, look out it was time for man and beast to clear out. He would take the bonnet and hit the tractor uttering these by now familiar word's "I'm sorry I sold the horse" as he kicked and booted the tractor.

Then my mum would say "give me a wee shot Alick" then dad would say "och what can you do woman It just won't start, you needn't bother", then he'd vanish off behind the shed to light up a Capstan. Thank goodness he smoked I would hate to think what like he would be without the old pacifiers. My mother and I would take turns with the handle, but it wasn't long before you got blisters on your hands. But mum was fly she would wrap her apron round the handle to prevent the blisters and although she was a small woman, she was very strong with all the hard work she was doing. When mum got the tractor started as she usually did (a woman's touch) dad would say "I think your mum has got the tractor started" and he'd suddenly appear back around the corner, having cooled off a bit after his cigarette. Dad would say "how did you manage to get her started Jesse" Och Alick you've got no patience."

Come on Loon he'd say better get some work done as onto the tractor he went. Poor dad never got the hang of clutch control, nobody ever showed him. His foot came straight of the pedal and the tractor took off with a sudden jerk. One had to be careful if you were standing on the trailer, you really had to hold on till he got going or you would end up overboard, very dangerous. He never gave me a shot of his tractor at first, well not very often until he found out it was ok going forward but going backwards with a trailer was a different matter. Dad would sometimes be shunting back and forwards for ages, then finally he would say "do you want a shot Loon" I was taught how to reverse a trailer so I was ok with that.

Another time we were lifting the tatties, we had this old spinner digger and halfway up the drill he had to stop to clear a choke of tattie shaws. He scraped them clear, hopped onto the tractor and took off with the usual jerk, breaking one of the drawbar pins. Dad took off sailing up the drill with the digger left behind. He'd travelled a good few yards until he turned round to see what was going on behind, when he realised the digger was no longer hitched to the tractor he started shouting "whoa whoa stop stop stop "Dad was all arms and legs as he flailed about to stop the tractor, he forgot he was on a tractor and not a pair of horse. He looked over at me and said "why did you not shout boy "and then he saw the funny side of it and he burst out laughing. I didn't laugh, because if I did, he would have said "it's not a laughing matter".

As the tractor got older it needed a wee bit of maintenance, which we couldn't really afford, the brakes were almost non-existent, they would just hold you on the flat but you couldn't stop on a brae. Then it was clutch trouble, when you pressed the clutch pedal nothing happened for about five or six seconds. I used to stand on the clutch well before I had to stop. One day I came home and there was no sign of dad or the tractor. I asked mum where dad was, she said "oh he's out the back sorting the tractor shed" he drove the tractor straight through the end of the shed. I took a wee peek around the corner and sure enough there was no end to the shed, just pieces of splintered wood and some bent and twisted sheets of corrugated iron. The tractor was wedged amongst some small shrubs. I made myself scarce for the rest of the afternoon this was one tractor repair that had to be done, and I remember Tom Macmillan coming out the next day to sort the clutch. Tom and his boys were very good to us on the croft, a really nice family, we would have been really lost without them.

Despite the arrival of the tractor there was still plenty of manual work to do. The Byres and the stables had to be mucked out. The dung was graiped onto the trailer and spread on the fields by hand graipe. The hay rucks were taken into the stack yard by putting a rope around the base and dragging them along. My dad used to fork the hay up to either my mum or i. It was mostly me that was on the stack and we had to pack it in such a way so as to make the stack watertight. It got really wobbly the further up you went, it's a wonder we never fell off and broke our necks. That's what happened to Andy's grandpa, he was up on a trailer load of straw and he lifted his arms to wave to a passerby, lost his balance, fell of the trailer, and broke his neck.

As I probably said before, mum wore mostly rags to keep her warm and also padding for any knocks or falls. There was no point in wearing good clothes. They would only get ruined with the croft work. My late wife Dot used to say "mum was never fat it was all those clothes she wore.

(Top, my sister Nan and I at Dunain. Bottom,
my old pal Jimmy on the left Roddy Main center
and me I had a plaster cast on at the time)

My dad I found, was growing increasingly harder on me. I would come home from school straight out to work, when all the other kids were playing, no time for play and sometimes I would get a good hiding if things went wrong. Things like the cows breaking into the turnip field. Knocking over a hay ruck or some implement would get broken. It was always my fault, sometimes mum could see I'd had enough and she would say "look it was me who did this" or that, then she got the row. Mostly my sister Nan was out of the picture as she had her job at Raigmore and then Dunain house. I had left school and one day mum said to me "you always wanted to join the air force, if I were you Jimmuck I would clear off, there's not much of a life here for you" but I couldn't go, the ties that held me to my dear mum seemed to tighten tighter than ever and I didn't go. I couldn't leave my mum to face all the hardship on her own. Many years later, she told me how grateful she was, but said you should have still left. The nearest I got was buying a suitcase, but it was never used.

On leaving the Highschool I got a job with Dochfour estates forestry, most of the locals and some former teachers were quite dismayed to say the least, that I should take a job as lowly as a forestry worker. They thought I was cut out for better things. This made me feel very uncomfortable and I used to try and hide my old piece bag on my way to work. Well, I wasn't used to working at an inside job and an elderly friend of mine cheered me up no end when I told him he said Jim "what a brilliant job outdoors, healthy fresh air and it would keep me fit, which it certainly did. No chainsaws in those days, all axe work, which I loved and cross cut saws.

A story which I must tell you and which spread through the whole estate like wildfire, happened one day at the sawmill yard, all of my fellow workers were a lot older than I, some were local but a good few came from the western islands. I got on really well with them all, but my favourite was big Barney the saw miller. A gentle Giant of a man and a voice to match his stature, one always knew when Barney was around you could hear his great hearty laugh and booming voice over the whine of the big Yankee circular saw which was responsible for the loss of two or three of his fingers. He always said "you can't call yourself a proper saw miller until you have lost a finger".

This day we were really busy and a wee bit behind schedule, Barney asked me to go with Ewan MacKinnon and give him a hand to light the fire, which heated the wood preservative boiler. The boiler was situated in a pit some seven or eight foot below ground level. The wood preservative was called celcure and had to be boiled then pressurised in a great long tank, so I followed Ewan over to the boiler. Ewan was a nice man, but very dour and easily annoyed, which I was soon to find out.

Ewan climbed down a rickety old ladder then told me to hand down some long dry sticks that he had prepared earlier up top. I handed him down two or three at a time then Ewan shouted up "throw me four or five down at a time or we'll never get this fire lit" so I did just that but this time one of the sticks slipped (and you'll never believe this but I can see it, as if it happened yesterday) Ewan had an old saucepan up top filled with creosote.

which is very flammable, to help start the fire? The stick swung round and hit the pan handle coping its entire contents all over Ewan. Well, if I never see rage again, I saw it that day on Ewan's face. He swore and he cursed "you little effing *** wait till I get up out of here I'll knock your head of your shoulders".

I was young at the time just sixteen and I had an awful habit of bursting out laughing for no apparent reason at times I don't know why because most of the time I generally had nothing to laugh about. It was a nervous thing which I eventually grew out of, but that day I just laughed and laughed at him oh I couldn't help myself. Even clambered up the rickety ladder and out of the pit like a great monster from the deep and I soon stopped laughing as he made a mad lunge at me, I wasn't hanging about, no sir, if he had caught me, I think he would have knocked my head off my shoulders.

He kept edging towards me and I was fast running out of space as the sawmill wall was not far behind me. There must have been some commotion as big Barney came on the scene "what the hell is going on here" he bellowed "have you not got that fire lit yet". Then Ewen turned around his whole front dripping with the black creosote, the only thing you could see through the black were the whites of his eyes and his teeth as he snarled at me. Oh boy then Barney took a fit and burst out laughing and he had to walk away. He said to the rest of the sawmill boys "for petes sake, don't go over there near the boiler. Ewan is going about like a raging bull covered from head to toe in creosote.

As he calmed down, just a wee bit I tried to get closer just to apologise but he still had aims at making a lunge for me, so I kept my distance. Then Ewan said "just you wait matey till my wife gets her hands on you, you'll not be laughing then, you little fart" and with that he rolled up his dungarees and he said "it's not only that but look at these, they're a brand new pair of long johns the wife just bought last Saturday, I just put them on today" you could see the lovely new white cotton at the knees fade into the black creosote just like a pair of wellington boots.

The Halloween party was due to be held in the local hall at the weekend and almost everyone on the estate went to that. It was a great family occasion. Where one could meet up with people that hadn't seen each other for some time. First there was a party for the school children and then after a dance, ceilidh for the grown-ups.

Ewan wasn't letting go, he said "my wife will be there at the party and you'll get what for, just you wait matey" I could still hear Barney laughing in the sawmill as he was telling the boys what had happened. Ewan trudged over to the works garage trying as best he could to keep his trouser legs away from his skin. Poor Ewan, creosote burns the skin and can be quite nasty, I think he must have borrowed a spare pair of overalls from Jim Lawson the mechanic.

When I went over to Barney, he said to me "what made Ewan worse was the fact you kept laughing at him, you shouldn't have laughed at him. That made him more enraged" and with that Barney himself broke into an uncontrolled fit of laughter. We all laughed for the rest of the afternoon and many more afternoons after that well all except poor Ewan.

As I write this, I find myself thinking that there is nobody about now to tell these tales as they have all gone home, I am the last of them. The last of the BlackFolders. As I said before I was only sixteen and the rest of my work mates were in their fifties.

Oh by the way I didn't go to the Halloween party that weekend and I was so looking forward to it. A few days later at home my dad said to me "did you cope a pan of creosote over auld Ewan "he said it's all round the estate. He was really wild at me and said "you better buy him a new pair of drawers, he had to throw the dirty ones away". I think I gave my mum money to buy a new pair which she bought from Cameron's on Church Street but my mind is a bit foggy on this one. I often wonder what the conversation was like when Ewan went home.

There is a row of Lombardy poplar trees growing alongside the main road from Dochgarroch school down to the entrance to the Caledonian canal locks and Loch Ness by Jacobite. When I worked on Dochfour in the early sixties Lachie Campbell our foreman, John Mackay and my old pal Ewan planted these trees. John never tired of telling me to get a better job, he was always complaining about the job and he thought I should get an easier job.

I'll always remember Lachie saying to me "och don't listen to John in years to come you'll be able to say, see those trees standing there, I planted them" and so it transpired I've told many people that story. They came from a nursery in Forres and were about six feet tall when planting. Now they are well over 100ft tall and you can see them swaying majestically in the breeze along the roadside to the old Dochgarroch school and down to AnTalla.

I worked every Saturday morning on Dochfour Estate forestry it was a forty-four-hour week for me. I was sixteen at this time and that would make the year 1960 a most memorable year in my life but unfortunately not for the right reasons. Saturday afternoon was a choice day for lifting the tatties as most people were free from work including the school children. There were quite a few lifters came that afternoon and things went very well, there was a bumper crop. Come lousing time all the bags had to be carted home to the barn, my dad told me to hitch the mare into the cart so I backed Polly into the cart and set off to pick up the bags. We had a few horses in our day, but Polly what a horse she was for farting and she gave me one of the reddest faces I ever got as I was leading her by the bridal every step, she took she farted, there were women there. Moira my old school friend and her pal amongst them.

Polly went, plod fart, plod fart, plod fart all the way to the top and when she reached the top and stood still, like a great giant steam engine, she let go one huge ripsnorter, I wished the ground would have opened and swallowed me up, what an embarrassment, I hoped they didn't think it was me.

That afternoon changed the whole course of my life, the tatties were in canvas sacks and some were way, way to full well over a c.w.t in most of them and the cart was quite a high lift. I started lifting the bags onto the cart and I came to this really full one, a guy called Specky had filled this one, rather than go and fetch another sack he'd filled this one to the brim. I managed to get it up onto the edge of the cart, but I couldn't lift it further with my arms so I gave it a push up with my right knee as hard as I could. I felt this searing tearing pain in my left hip and a burning sensation all the way down my leg. The grownups were all having a smoke and a blether, but mum had noticed what had happened and said to dad "James is not fit to be lifting these heavy bags on his own, can't you see he's struggling" Then dad shouted over "wait a minute loon, we'll give you a hand that's a job for two" but for me it was too late, the damage had been done I'll never forget that day the memory of that ripping pain has lived with me all my life.

I struggled with the pain for a long time, bending was excruciating. Mum had great sympathy for me, but dad hard as ever "och it's only a sore back, he's lucky that's all he's got to worry about". My sister Nan used to put my socks on and tie my shoes and boots.

I still went to work at Dochgarroch but Mr. Nicol the head Forrester noticed I was in pain and took me in to the doctors all he gave me were painkillers, which didn't help much. Then one day at work I hurt my back worse if that was possible, lifting a log on my shoulder. Mr. Nicol took me home that day, I then saw the doctor who referred me to Raigmore and of course I was hospitalised. The doctor put me on traction for a week or so. Bandages on my legs and weights and pulleys suspended on them. What an utter load of nonsense the pain was getting worse, when the traction was stopped, I was put in plaster from my neck to my hips this went on for nearly two years and I was not getting any better. Every time I went back to the hospital, they would keep me in and put a new plaster on, the last one was the final straw it was called a spica, it went from my neck down to my left knee, keeping me in a straight rigid position, of course I wasn't able to work and my dad would say "when are you getting that plaster off".

I remember the last plaster I got on. It was put on by a lovely kind woman sister Gordon, I'll never forget her. She took me aside and told me that they were planning to cut me open and put a new hip joint in. She said "you're only a young boy, you don't want these people cutting you up. They don't know what they're doing when it comes to bones, you'll be ruined for life". Next time she said "when they cut your plaster off tell them that you are better and the pain has gone. Then get yourself down to an osteopath, a certain Mr. Fuchs who had a practice at 4 Alby Terrace Aberdeen, I'll even go with you". So that's what I did. When I went in for my appointment, they put me on a bed and cut the plaster off me, the Surgeon said," now see if you can touch your toes. I could still feel the pain and it took me all my time to stop shouting out, I told them I was fine and free from pain. They ordered me a surgical corset from Hogg and Ross and a supply of painkillers and sent me home.

I was expecting an ambulance home as that was what took me there but no, I had to make my own way home. With me being so long in plaster my whole body felt like jelly, I was staggering all over the place, my muscles were so weak as my body had depended on the plaster for support for so long

Soon after my dad took me down to Aberdeen to see Mr. Fuchs. Mr. Fuchs knew right away just by looking at me what the problem was. I had a habit in fact I always stood with most of my weight on my right leg, very lop sided, he said to dad "your son's left leg is completely out of the hip socket it is about 1 ½ "longer than his right one." I remember thinking oh dear he won't be able to do anything about that. Mr Fuchs asked me about the hospital and the doctors there. He said "I've lost count the number of people who come from there to see me, you would not believe. They are so excellent'. at other problems, but bones are a specialist thing. He lifted me up onto his orthopedic bed, I didn't even have to take my shirt off and he proceeded to work and twist me about. I remember quite vividly him asking me what the weather was like in Inverness and just as I was about to answer he gave me such an awful twist. I felt a sharp pain and heard a loud crack and he continued for another fifteen minutes or so. There were bones and joints out all over my body, especially my neck which he put back into place by rolling my head to and fro.

When he was finished, he asked me to stretch down and touch my toes, I said to him I can't "try" he said I stretched down and to my complete and utter disbelief I touched my toes, the pain had completely gone. Two and half years of agony gone in just under half an hour. I don't think I felt such relief, happiness emotion in my whole life as I did that afternoon. Now I could put my own shoes and socks on. I could bend to tie my laces. I could do anything, I had to be very careful, what I did with my hip been out of joint for so long. I could work again. He charged my dad £2- 10/- OR £2.50 which was half his usual fee as I was just eighteen. That was definitely the best £2.50 that my dad ever spent.

We left Mr. Fuchs and I remember my dad saying to

me "do you fancy a cup of tea James" he was so nice to me that day. I thought to myself why dad can't be more like that more of the time. We went into this café and sat down we were there for ages and no waiters came to serve us. Then dad said "I think this is a help yourself place" so dad went and came back with two teas and two sandwiches, two yokels down from the hills. I'd never been in a café before apart from going to Burnetts café with my mum when I was very young.

When we returned home, I started feeling my way about again. Then one day Mr. Nicol the head forester came to my door and asked me if I would like to go to the forestry college down in argyle as I had already done my practical, I thanked him but I never took him up on his offer.

As I didn't want to go back into forestry, my mum told me to seek a lighter job. I applied for a position as a costing clerk with Rossleigh, the main garage in town which turned out to be successful. Didn't really fancy the job inside all of the time, making out repair bills, warranty claims, estimating accident damage etc but it was a good clean job I suppose, but at nights and weekends I helped out on the croft as usual.

One of my friends and favourite people who I met was a great guy called Hugh Reid but everybody just called him Lofty, he was an ex guardsman in the British army and he ran a small fencing contractor business. Lofty found himself with quite a backlog of work and he approached me with a view to employment which I gratefully accepted. This was a welcome source of extra income which helped keep the croft running and also my own wee nights out, busking in the pubs and clubs.

Hard work was never a chore with Lofty, the craic was brilliant and many a happy day we spent erecting stock and deer fences on hill and dale.

My next friend was a Davy Nicol who had just returned from agricultural college at Aberdeen and he started work with Lofty and i.

Lofty lived with his brother Jimmy and his wife Lou and two boys in a beautiful log cabin above Lochend with a full view of Loch Ness. It was built to a very high standard by Eddie Hunter a tobacconist who had a shop in Inglis street, I recall. One day Lofty called Dave and I into the house and he said "sit down boys I've something to tell you, I've decided to pack up and leave Lochend to go to Achterarder and start a life anew". This was a big shock to me I thought Lofty would always be around us here in the Highlands. A sudden tinge of sadness entered me; I was losing all my old pals.

"Well boys" Lofty said "I'm leaving the business to the two of you" and it was a good business. We also did building work draining, woodland clearance really anything that people needed doing. So, here was another chapter of my life.

Davys wife Gwen was a brilliant little singer and she and I formed the singing duo Simply Jimmy and Gwen. Apart from our stints in the old Northern hotel and the Academy bar we played at many venues in and all-around town. We played at the opening of the newly built Hay loft in Eastgate for Provost Grigors son Robbie if I recall correctly. Then we played at the grand opening of the newly refurbished Abertarff in Academy Street. Things were looking up also with Gwen's popularity there were gigs in the British legion and most other places in town. But we finally committed ourselves to the Abertaff, it was handy not having to shift our heavy gear every night.

David and I worked all over the North erecting cattle and deer fences for estates and farms. My mum kept the croft running and I did all the groundwork ploughing etc at nights and weekends. While I was fencing up at Loch Broom just across the Corrieshalloch gorge for a local farmer a Mr. Renwick that I found one of the best friends I ever had a little black and tan collie pup, I hadn't long lost my old black Labrador "Rover" and I was looking for a pup, and lo and behold one of Mr. Renwick's collie bitches had just had pups and there were two left out of the litter. One morning Mr. Renwick came out of the kennel with the two little pups in the palm of his hand, he said "just take your pick" so I chose one.

The pup was too young to leave his mother at this stage so I had to return to Loch Broom several weeks later when the pup was weaned. I took him home and in no time at all my mum had him house trained; she was an expert at this. All our dogs and cats kept the house clean, they always asked out. We called our new pup "Lucky" but sometimes he got called Lachy. He was a brilliant sheepdog and companion, I enjoyed some of the happiest days of my life with him. He made our life so much easier, if you wanted to catch a ewe or lamb for marking or checking I would just point the sheep out and he had an uncanny knack of coping him over pinning it down till I arrived.

He went everywhere with me, he loved to pop onto the tractor, for he knew he was going for a jaunt, maybe into town or the sawmill for wood or many other places. He wouldn't let anyone near the tractor when I was away from it. He would sit and guard my jacket or jersey if I left it unattended, such a faithful dog. He watched every move I made as he would lie asleep on the floor beside me. He would keep opening his eyes every two or three minutes to see if I was still there. He was a great dog for chasing the birds. Mum trained him to chase the crows away from the crops and he spent hours chasing the swallow's as they swooped down and skimmed alongside him. He could run like the wind he was a match for a full-grown hare on a level field.

One day I was stacking bales up in the top field, I was a smoker at the time and I tucked my pack of cigarettes in between the bales to stop them getting crushed in my pocket. I finished that field and we went down to the lower field to stack the bales there. When we got there, I felt in my pocket for a cigarette and then I remembered that I had left them way up in the top field. I said to Lucky "go and get my cigarettes, go and get my cigarettes go" he then ran up the hill and out of sight, several minutes later he ran back with them in his mouth and they weren't even crushed. I'd often played with him and an empty cigarette packet so he knew what I meant.

My mum would always give him a big stick to take home for the fire and some were big sticks, he seldom came home without one. My mum used to love it when I took my guitar out and sing "Hello Mary Lou", Lucky would join in and wail his way right to the end, but he really didn't bother accompanying me with any other songs just "Mary Lou". He was a great gun dog as well, he loved going out with the gun after various sorts of vermin.

The Fencing was going very well and we employed two men who were well experienced at the fencing and most country matters like ditching, dry stone walling and sheepherding, what a pair of worthiness. Well hardened to the old crater and a bottle or two of Guinness. Duncan Macleod stayed in digs in town, but big Dan wanted to stay in our old barn, if he only knew what went on in there, I don't think he would have been quite so keen. It must have been freezing out there especially in the winter. Every weekend Big Dan would hit town. He was a powder monkey, a shot blaster and had worked a lot with the Irish paddy's (as he called them) on the hydroelectric dams and tunnels. He had acquired a lot of their lingo, mannerisms, and habits least of all his Guinness to wash down his whisky every Sunday mornings when you went out to the barn there was usually a big cardboard sign pinned to the door which read "DO NOT DISTURB". My mum grew very fond of Big Dan he was really a lovely guy but the demon drink was his downfall. Then Dan moved up in the world he managed to save up enough money to buy a caravan, he was so proud of this van. One Sunday morning Big Dan came to our door this was him just coming home. I had been out myself that night and was still in my bed so my mum answered the door. "Is Jim in Mrs. Johnston" asked Dan. He always called my mum Mrs. Johnston when he had a good shot for that was his last landlady's name "no dear" mum said "he's still in his bed, what's wrong"   "oh" said Dan "I was just wanting to borrow a hacksaw to cut the lock on the caravan door, I lost my keys last night". My mum gave him a hacksaw but t wasn't sharp enough to cut the padlock, so big Dan smashed one of the windows got in and boarded it up. He managed to unscrew the lock from the inside, this happened every other week and eventually there were no more windows to break, just the skylight which was left alone as it was too narrow for big Dan to slip through. I said to Dan "Don't take the keys with you hang them up in the tractor shed". "oh, somebody might steal them there" he said what could I say to that. Then he bought a wee crowbar to bust the padlocks every time he lost his keys. It was so funny eventually there was a pile of broken padlocks underneath the caravan.

A few months passed and Duncan got a caravan and he decided he wanted to stay on the croft. So, he pitched his caravan next to Dans they were good friends, but always falling out when they had a dram, very argumentative.

One day big Dan came to see my mum and he told her, he had enough of everything in general "I'm away back to Ireland, that's where my heart is". So, next day a low loader came to take Danny's caravan away. He threw his arms up around my mum and thanked her for everything. It was a sad tearful farewell. As the caravan slowly disappeared up the big brae and around the corner mum said "ahh that's the last we'll see of poor Danny".

The weekend passed and Duncan came to see us. He said big Dan's caravan is in at Clachnaharry just six miles from the croft, it's parked in MacLeod's caravan park right opposite the Inn, which he was in all weekend. Danny got a job at Ladystone farm, just a few miles along the road. The farmer came with his tractor and towed his van up to the farm. Big Dan was such a character I could probably write a whole book in itself about him. Danny bought himself a little van, a recipe for disaster if ever there was one. There were two elderly brothers living in the old toll house at Clachnaharry and someone passed by the toll house on their way to Ladystone farm "I see the brothers at the old toll house have got a van" Tom said, that can't be, the brothers don't drive "well there's a van in their garden this morning" said the passer by. Tom asked "what make and colour is it" small brown Vauxhall was the reply "ach that's big Dans van, I wondered why he never came home last night". Danny had crashed through the fence and into the garden on his way home to Ladystone farm.

Another night and this takes some believing, but if you knew Dan there's nothing that he would do that you couldn't believe. He actually ended up on the railway line and drove for about half a mile along it, eventually stalling the engine as the van got stuck between the rails. How an earth he got there, nobody knows, not even big Dan. This was a near disaster for if it was through the day the train would be running. Someone who knew Tom phoned him and told him about the van and he rushed down with the tractor and towed the van home. Tom said "Danny for your own good and others I'm going to take the van keys off you at the weekends". Danny thought that was a good idea, he later said to me "I couldn't understand why the road was so bumpy". Poor Danny he ended up at Balloan farm and one winter morning the farmer came to see why he was not around and found him dead, sitting by the fireside with a bottle of his fav Guinness at his feet. He never made it back to his favourite land of forty shades of green poor Danny.

Andy my old pal and neighbour lived on a farm about a mile away. Whenever I could, I would make my way down to his house with my guitar strapped on my back and a bottle of this and a bottle of that in the other hand, but a wee bit more of this than that.

There was always a ceilidh or nearly always a ceilidh going on, a very musical family. These ceilidh's lasted well into the next day and sometimes beyond and often we didn't know if it was the dawn breaking or the twilight. Andy's brother Malcolm was a star player, non-better on the old red three row accordion. Andy's brother Malcolm played the Irish circuit where there was and still is a demand for Scottish accordion music and when he came home on holiday that was something to really look forward to. Aye the parties at Andy's were legendary, his dad Ian was some character an accordionist of no mean repute himself especially on the wee two row box. I'll never forget, oh will I ever forget the day we went to Largs to hear Malcolm playing in the theatre. Ian had heard that my sister Nan had passed her driving test just a few weeks earlier.

Poor Nan was not very keen as she had taken seven attempts to pass her driving test, but I managed to persuade her to take Ian and I down to Largs. What a nightmare this turned out to be, I could never go through anything like that again in my life again, many moons ago over fifty years actually, I wrote a song about it and here it is. Ian just absolutely loved this song.

(THE DAY WE WENT TO LARGS, TO THE TUNE OF CAPTAIN CARSWELL)

Andy and I played a lot of gigs together way back then. My mum I recall used to say "the two of you are as good as any of the groups you see on TV" but I didn't take any notice of poor mum. She was very musical herself, on reflection I regret not teaming up together. We were young and carefree, Andy got married and I found myself in a serious relationship, and we decided to go our separate ways. Again, it would be a long time, way too long before we met up again. Andy travelled abroad and with his slim Whitman, Marty Robbins style soon became a very popular entertainer in the clubs and bars of Spain, Portugal, Florida, and some of the cruise ships. I suppose he was just a notch away from being up there with the best of them.

Working on the croft my mum and I were inseparable working alongside each other in all sorts of weather. Dad went back to work on the estate from time to time and did most of the tractor work, when he could get it started. In the meantime, aunty Belle had moved up from Blackpool with Uncle Jack and her two boys and a girl. They moved into a little cottage just next door to us. One day whilst returning from town Aunty Belle called me over as I had passed by her cottage, she told me that Dr Barlow was out to see dad and that he was diagnosed with bowel cancer and that he had left it rather too late to see about it. What could I say I felt numb? A long time ago dad was taking funny turns and wanting to go to the loo all the time. One night he went rushing outside clutching his stomach, I followed him out and he was leaning against the outside wall. I plucked up the courage and said to him "look dad, I'm going to get the doctor for you" "there's no doctor coming here boy, who's going to look after this croft". Eventually dad was taken into the infirmary given a colostomy and a six-year life expectancy and that really was the end of his crofting days. So sad to see a strong fit man cut down more or less in the prime of his life to that scourge of all scourges. Mum and I were now really on our own and suddenly we enjoyed our newfound freedom that we hadn't known before. However, dad got out of hospital after several months and he recovered quite well. He started to develop the garden in front of the house and did a tremendous job but he left the croft work for mum and I. Meanwhile the croft was still going strong but my dad took a turn for the worse the cancer had returned and with a vengeance. Mum had now to look after dad, she would not put him into care. Dad kept telling her "please Jessie don't put me in a home" and she kept her promise to him despite a tremendous burden on her, a burden she said she was born to carry. Dad was in terrible pain his whole body was being eaten away by this scourge of a thing and my mum had to dress him constantly. She used to say that she was put on this earth for a purpose, first to come back from London to nurse John Blackfold and now to nurse her husband. It was terrible to watch, I would often come in and she would be crying, but I knew she didn't want me to see her crying so I used to creep back out. It really was almost too much for her, hardy soul that she was. She got her strength from the Lord she said, mum had a great unshakeable faith. Dad used to say "I wish I was out of it; I just want to be with the Lord".

Towards the end one·night mum and I were sitting by a roaring fire and dad was laid up in the bed that the NHS had supplied. Dad said to mum "Put the devil on the fire Mum looked at me and I picked up the shovel and went through the motions of putting something on the fire Ah that's much better now James said dad

When I was in my early twenties I started going to the old Northern hotel, run by a great gentleman Duncan Grant, with whom I became very friendly with and joined the darts team. After a while Duncan got to know I played the guitar a wee bit and said to me "it's awful dull in the lounge upstairs, do you think yourself and a girl singer could come in at weekends and liven the place up a bit" oh Duncan I said I don't think I can manage that. However, my pal David's wife was a brilliant wee singer and David said "Gwen is all up for it and it will be a few extra bob for us" and so started another chapter in my life. We played there for a number of years and had some rare old times. The lounge was like a large dining room and there were an assortment of all kinds of chairs, arm chairs etc some of the punters had their own special chairs. In·between times Gwen and I played at wedding parties and other bars. Then we got some sad news Duncan had decided to give up the Northern hotel. What a big blow that was for Gwen and I, it was so much a part of our lives.

I really enjoyed playing in the Northern hotel. The lounge upstairs was a cosy place to sit and have a wee dram. Most people were very friendly, I made a lot of good friends there. Sadly, most are gone from this planet.

Even so there was the occasional ruckus, Gwen my partner was great for the Irish songs she had quite a repertoire, but I had no idea that an Irish song could affect some people as it did this night. The merry ploughboy was one of Gwen's favorites songs and she was belting it out. A small company at the bar were getting quite angry and shouted at us to stop singing this rebel song. This made Gwen sing louder and stronger, she was a wee tough warrior, next minute a heavy glass ashtray came hurtling across the room, it broke in two and part of it embedded in the door behind me, just missing my head. Some of the guy's pals and the barman restrained the fellow. Eventually the police came on the scene and order was restored. Duncan the boss then came over and told us to carry on but no more Irish songs. But she still sang the old, rugged cross, the old bog road, forty shades of green and many more. I don't know how she managed to learn them all. You never knew who was going to come into the Northern. One night this huge guy dressed up as a Norseman horned helmet, sword and shield came in. strode up to the bar and ordered a lager. He was going around the bars in town promoting this new Norseman lager. It turned out he was Fred Nosher Powell a leading contender for the British heavy weight titles. He mixed in with the crowd and he even gave us a song. He left with the promise he would be back later for a party after closing time. Well, he did come back and we had some party that night. Norseman lager was on the house, Duncan the boss was so chuffed, that out of all the bars in town the Norseman decided to come back to the Northern. I don't know if the Norseman lager was a big hit, but it certainly was that night. Word soon got around that the Northern was closing and Alec Wheeler the bar manager at the old

Academy bar was looking for entertainers and he sent a scout Brucie Hendry and a partner to check Gwen and I out. Halfway through our gig Brucie came over and had a word with us and asked if we could play resident in the Academy bar lounge Friday and Saturday nights. We took him up on his offer and so started another chapter in our musical life. I made a lot of good friends in my time at the Northern and Academy bars, but sadly a lot of them have departed to pastures green. One of them was the barman Peter Macgregor, probably the smartest barman in town, always on the go with a dish towel over his shoulder. He used to keep his lighted cigarette behind his ear between puffs until it got too short and too hot. One night someone ordered a pack of cigars, which were kept on the far end of the bar on a high shelf. Peter came striding through from the public bar, reached up to grab the cigars and suddenly disappeared. Rosy the manageress said "where on earth did Peter go to". I looked over to the bar counter and there was poor Peter clambering up out of the cellar, somebody had left the trap door open and poor Peter had fallen straight through the floor. Fortunately, he was ok apart from a few small cuts. Once we found out Peter was ok, we all started laughing much to Peter's annoyance, but in the end even Peter saw the funny side, but no one ever admitted leaving the trap door open. Another time I was taking a wee break and this wee mannie, a real country yokel, wearing a blue tweed suit the ones that come back in fashion every twenty years or so and sporting a grey wax moustache. It was obvious he had a good shot in him, but he was out for more as he pushed and barged his way through to the front of the bar. He kept looking round behind him as he ordered a large Grouse, when next this big fat wifie, she probably worked at the local sawmill burst through the door. She shouted above the crowd "Don't serve that wee sod, he's had enough to drink" the place was jam packed that night in the public bar and the wee mannie being nice and slim made his escape through the crowd, but his wife as she turned out to be had a heck of a job getting out. I went back through the lounge after my break, and who do you think was there but the wee mannie himself. He had nipped out of the public bar walked a few yards and by sheer luck found himself in the lounge bar. He ordered his drink and looked around as much as to say I couldn't care two hoots she won't find me here in this crowd. He was just about to take a swig and of course who do you think came in but the big fat wifie herself. The wee mannie was much nearer the door this time and his wife was blocking his exit. He tried to make a run for it but with one hand she lifted him of the floor by the scruff of the neck and shouting at him "come on Wullie oot o here ya wee sod, we're going to miss the last ferry home to the Black Isle now". Well, they both disappeared out the door, I fully expected him to come back in again, but that was the last I ever saw of them. I don't know if they made the ferry home that night, but I would like to think that they did.

The old Academy bar had to close for refurbishment but I picked up various gigs. When Andy came home from time to time, weddings etc. Did a lot of gigs with the three Penny's dance band and odd jobs at the Clansman hotel. Then I got a regular gig Friday and

Saturday nights at the Coach House which led to some gigs at Thurso, Bettyhill ect.

When the old Academy opened it was renamed the Abertarff not just an old working man's bar but a modern up to date fully carpeted rather posh place. Big Frank was manager at that time and to my surprise he asked me if Gwen and I could get together again and play Friday and Saturday nights. This we did and on the opening night Frank said "you made front page of the Courier". Abertarff opening night, entertainment by Jimmy and Gwen, we were quite chuffed at that.

One night I remember in the old Academy my old mate Vicky came from the public bar through to the lounge, I hadn't started yet. He told me that he had a wee bet with the boys through in the bar. "The boys were all saying Jim always starts with Rick Nelsons Hello Mary Lou. I'll bet you he will", Vick said "I bet you a pint of lager each that he won't tonight" so Vick said "do us a wee favour, and start with another song, a Johnny cash one maybe". Vicky went back through and I started off with I'll Walk The Line, at the corner of my eye I saw Vicky peering through the hatch, with a big grin on his face. I don't know if the boys ever found out.

Gwen and I finished, of course in the good old days when our gig was over, there was never a shortage of parties, it wasn't so much of a question is there a party on tonight but where is the party tonight. These parties led to a sad chapter in my life, Gwen's husband David, my best friend at the time thought that it was time to call it a day as Gwen loved her parties too and things were getting hectic at this time, so we decided to split up. It was a big wrench, we'd been together for a long time and it was always Jimmy and Gwen, now it would be just Jim.

Gwen said to me are you going to pack it in now I don't think you'll manage by yourself. She once told me do you know this Jim if you weren't so shy you would go all the way to the top, but I never ever had that confidence it was drummed out of me when I was young, I never forgot her words. Poor Gwen she is long gone now she passed away many moons ago her husband David died a few years after and they are both buried in a little hilly graveyard at Auldearn, which reminds me of one of Gwen's and I's favourite songs, the song is called The Long Black Veil if you listen to it, it might explain a few things.

(Myself and my wife Dot)

(Building the bungalow)

(The old croft house at Dunain)

(My son Jamie with his old Astra GTE)

It was in the old Academy bar that I met Dot, my future wife, she came in a few times with her friend and one night I asked her if she fancied a Chinese after I had finished my Gig. I remembered going to the Chinese, Dot and her pal and I and halfway through the meal I asked her if she would go out with me next week. She said, "wait till you hear how many kids I've got you'll soon change your mind". Poor Dot she had a hard time of it a broken marriage and a failing relationship I said it doesn't matter tongue in cheek, she said without looking at me" I've got five", I nearly choked on my chicken nugget. "oh" I said, "that doesn't matter" and so it began for the two of us, a close but very stormy relationship. But we weathered all sort of storms the two of us, the sort of things that you would only see in the movies. So now Dot was a regular with me but she didn't sing parties were all the rage after pub hours and this time another old friend Vicky (some character) invited us round to his house for a few drams and a sing song, I don't know how many came round but Vicky was a wee bit short on the seating department he went through the back and he said to Dot "I'll give you the good chair it's got three legs" and he propped it up with books and magazines and Dot had her seat. Then he said to me "you're playing the guitar so I'll give you the next best chair" it had two front legs so he propped it up with its back to the wall and he said, "whatever you do don't lean forward or it will come away from the wall". He brought through another few chairs but he was fast running out of books and magazines to prop them up the chairs were result of many of the really wild party's that Vicky was notorious for but what happened next I think was Vicky's party piece he then said "Ah what about myself" and he went through the back and returned with a one legged chair he looked over at me gave me a wink and a big grin and said "its ok Jim im used to this one I always keep it for myself" he sat on the stool swaying from left then to the right and just when you thought the whole thing would collapse he would manage to push himself against the wall to steady the chair again. Can't remember going home that night. By now Dot and I were going great guns but I could have done without the guns and she was coming out to the croft whenever she could. Yvonne, Robbie, Steven, Laura and Sonia were all at school and she had to be home for them coming out at about four o'clock or so. Dot and I had a wee baby boy we called Jamie, then just over a year later Rory came along. We lived in the town at the time, I didn't like town life I've always been a county Yokel and always will. Jamie was fine a good healthy baby but poor Rory was not so strong he was very prone to fits and one day we had to rush him by Ambulance to hospital, he took six fits in quick succession we thought we had lost him, Doctors didn't know what was wrong, but it turned out Rory had severe learning difficulties but he pulled through it all and after a good number of years he grew out of the fits. I was wasting a lot of time travelling back and fore from the town so I talked to Dot about building a house. We would get financial assistance from the crofting commission. Dot shrugged the idea off saying that in the first place we would never be able to afford it plus other legal issues. However, I went ahead and got the finance in place, well most of it there are always extras that have to be paid for,

The usual loan from the bank etc I ordered a beautiful three bedroom kit house (a bungalow) from Walker Timber Boness for the princly sum of seven thousand pounds, goodness gracious where did these house prices disappear to, Then the magic day the kit house arrived it was on two great artics and they couldn't get down the narrow twisting roads so the house kit was unloaded at the farmhouse next door we had to cart it home bit by bit on the tractor and the trailer, this was a job within itself there seemed to be so many pieces and my budget wouldn't allow for much if any extra labour. However, we managed to get the kit down onto the field where it was to be built. As I laid the first corner block in place Dot was sitting in a pile of wood puffing away on her fag and she said to me "You'll never finish this house it will take you forever" I got all the founds laid nice and square and level, laid the base plate ready for the walls. I was selling my tatties to Jim Jackson Spar Grocers at the time and he had offered to give me a hand with the build so sure enough he came out and we had the walls up in a day or so. Then Jim said to me "whose giving you a hand with the rest of the house, I can only give you another day and I'm afraid I've a couple of houses myself". My heart sunk, how would I manage on my own with a project which seemed way beyond me, however Jim gave me a quick briefing on how to go about it. All the pieces I learned were all numbered so it was just a matter of fitting them in order. Jim came back with his pal to put the roof trusses up and then I was on my own. I had built shed's extensions all sort of wooden ornaments so I was quite handy with the tools plus I had watched my dad build several out houses on the croft and that served me in good stead, plus I always felt I got help from above "in straits a present aid". Most of the work I had to do myself as I couldn't afford to pay for much labour, but I did get a lot of good help at times from various sources. My friend at the time big Sandy was a top-notch electrician and he did all the wiring for me which was a huge thing. Dot's boys Robbie and Steve did what they could lifting up roof tiles etc and the house soon took shape. I had to do all the croft work at the same time along with my mum since dad died. Mum no longer had the chore of catching and milking the cows, I just left the calves suck their mothers, she was very glad of this change in operations as her hands were now bad with arthritis, plus all kind of accident damage. So, I had to get this bungalow built and run the croft at the same time but eventually after much toil, trouble and a huge expansion of my budget the house was finished, well almost there were always little bits and pieces to do. It was a three-bedroom bungalow I actually needed and wanted four but this was beyond my budget. There was a lovely big lounge with a roof to ceiling picture window, a roomy kitchen diner, bathroom and one bedroom had en-suite toilet. Then came the day when we moved in, we shifted everything with the tractor and trailer all the small stuff we took in the car. Dots five children Yvonne, Laura, Sonia, Robbie, Steve and my own two boys Jamie and Rory. Can't exactly remember the sleeping arrangements but we managed somehow.

To try and get us out of the bit Andy's dad Ian let me rent a 15 acres field on his farm, which I put under tatties this was fine until it came to lifting time. Poor

Dot I don't think she knew what she was letting herself into. I managed to get a few pickers, Big Roddy and old pal was an excellent worker, my mum, Dot and a few others we could have done with twenty-five or so pickers as the drills were way longer than on the croft, 600 yards or so. We worked till dusk each day we didn't stop for anything to eat; our main mission was to get the crop lifted before the frost came. I had no lights on the trailer for the main road/ Big Roddy sat on the back holding an old cycle lamp which gave off as much light as a fag end. We wouldn't get away with that nowadays. I had to build a new, much larger tattie shed which somehow, I managed to build that same year. The proceeds of the tattie sales helped to reduce my loan, just a wee bit. By the time I had paid for the new shed, seed tatties, fertiliser, paper bags, diesel, some labour charger plus house bills there was very little left over at the end of the day.

(Angus Grant on a very hard winter at Abricahan)

I slowly drifted away from the music scene for a short time apart from gigs at the coach house, crown court and various other venues. The rowdy more modern music was taking over. Country and western, Jim Reeves, Johnny Cash sort of stuff were not so popular with the new younger customers that were coming in to see this new Abertarff Bar however Dot got good part time work in The Clansman Hotel just a few miles up the road, situated just beside Loch Ness. After a couple of weeks John Mackenzie, the owner asked Dot if I would come up to play in the lounge bar at the weekends, as a lot of Caley cruising boats were pulling in at the harbour for some food, drink and entertainment so I said, "Ok I'll do it". My first night there I will always remember my amplifiers and speakers were stored out in the lean to and hadn't been used for a while, so I arrived at The Clansman set up my gear and started my gig. I had just finished my first song when John came over and said to me "there is an awful lot of wasps in here tonight" and then he noticed one coming out the back of the amplifier, I gingerly took a look inside ("I hate wasps") Gee Wizz there was a wasps pot built inside it, with the amplifier been stored outside in the lean to it was an ideal spot for a nest. We got rid of the wasps with some fly killer and that put an end to that. We were lucky that the pot was quite small and no one got stung.

One weekend at the Clansman John said to me jokingly "you'd better be on your best behavior next Saturday as the BBC cameras will be here to film a holiday ad for Cliff Michelmores holiday programme – Wish You Were Here." I was a wee bit excited but rather nervous at the thought of this, those dreaded nerves which became my constant companion through life but I've always managed to overcome them when the time came to perform. So, when Dot and I arrived that night, there was Cliff Michelmore sitting at the bar, John introduced us to him a very friendly down to earth kind of guy and we had a wee blether. So eventually I got started and mid evening, this disc jockey who was with the cameras came over and said to me "do you know who I am" I had to say "No" as I had not got a clue who he was he was taken quite a back as I learned later he was one of the top disc jockeys at the time, I still can't remember his name I think he thought I was winding him up but he was a really ok sort of guy. Then he asked me if he could plug the crews sound gear into mine saying "we'd like to do a wee clip of you for our TV programme" I said "I didn't mind" but he could see I was rather nervous. He came over to me and said "look Jim you will be ok, we will try not to focus too much on you" he asked me If I would mind singing a song I had sung earlier "Hank Snows" Southbound which was one of my favourites anyway and away I went. The programme was shown not long after and Dot taped it on the old video recorder. I was quite chuffed as friends and relations were phoning Dot "I was on nightshift at McDermott's at the time" saying "Did you see Jim on tv tonight" nowadays I suppose it's not a big thing to be on the tv but back then it was quite the thing to be on the tv.

One night not long after Dot wanted to show her video to her sister Laura but we couldn't find it, well we did but Sonia used the tape to record Top of the Pops which she did every week and she had taped over it, she just grabbed the first tape and put it on and my only claim to fame vanished like a rat down a drainpipe. I never forgave her for that, well I did sort of, well of course I did. Around about 1985 divers had found a WWII wellington bomber which had crashed into the loch during the war, I won't go into much detail here as it is well documented. It was decided to raise the bomber for restoration and there was a hive of activity going on for a good number of weeks the press tv crews, local reports plus the salvage crews were all staying at The Clansman hotel and Dot was exceptionally busy at this time. There was a fixed budget for the operation as some of the pretty high-tech gear was wanted for other work so there was a big rush at the latter end to complete the task. Some reporters were anxious to get photos of the actual lift and they asked me if I knew where they could get a boat to take them to the bomber site. A local worthy and a very good friend of mine Angus Grant who had a croft up at Abriachan just beyond The Clansman was sipping away at his whisky overheard the conversation. "I'm just the man you're looking for" piped Angus. "I've got a boat I'll take you out" it was late at night and very dark then Angus said to me like only a highland crofter could say "Jim will you come with us to hold the torch for us and we'll need some help to bale the water out of the old tub. The reporters looked at each other in amazement they were obviously expecting a nice fancy boat, not an old rusty tub that Angus had.

They climbed very gingerly aboard with all their fancy gear and equipment. One guy who was shaking a wee bit said to Angus "I don't see any life buoys" Oh said Angus "you'll see them soon enough if we start sinking, they'll float up to us. They're down below out of the way at the moment". I didn't go with Angus as I had to finish my gig for John so we parted company on the shore, a rather strange eerie sight. Just a coal black shadow and a wee torch beam shining out into the dark water of Loch Ness. Towards midnight Angus and the crew returned to the clansman although frozen to the marrow they had all made it safely there and back. A few of them must have thought it was a one-way ticket they had bought but as the reporters were beginning to thaw out and the whisky started to take effect. Angus had suddenly got one of the best boats they had ever seen

Angus's boat was suddenly transformed from being a rusty old tub into a great and wonderful ship. It had done its job all the press got the shots they had wanted, and they all lived happily ever after especially Angus as he tucked a wee wad of notes into his back pocket.

(Yvonne, Rory with Joey Andrews old
house in the background)

(Mum on a tractor)

My mum was a very religious woman. She never tired of telling me how blessed she was and how good the Lord was to her even through the many ups but much more many downs. Every time she got hurt and there were more than a few, she would say "ach look Jimuck your meant to get your knocks and bruises, you just can't sail through life wrapped in cotton wool, whilst on about mum's faith I must tell you this story.

On the croft there was a very nasty steep brae dividing the lower and upper fields. This brae was feared by all and Sundry. Andy's dad was forever on about it. But we had to get to the lower fields and back up. There was an alternative route which meant taking a long detour and the tractor was not licenced for road use at the time. It was sometimes a hit or miss if you made it to the top especially if it was wet and slippery, and the load a wee bit too heavy. If you got stuck halfway up you were in big trouble, the weight of the trailer could drag you back over the edge and capsize.

I had acquired an old ex-army Austin Champ a 4 x 4 with a huge Rolls Royce power unit. We used it a lot when we were at the fencing to carry all the materials out on the hills. This machine would go almost anywhere even places you could hardly walk to. One day mum and I put a really big load of sheaves to save us going back a second time. Mum said you'll never get up the big brae with that load on, we should have split it in two let me off at the foot of the hill and I'll walk up to the top. I revved the Champ up and made a charge at the brae she was slipping and spinning but searching and finding a good grip between the stones. I happened to look down at the field below and there was my poor dear mum on her knees on the wet ground, her wizened old hands clasped in prayer, what a faith she had. I knew then that I was going to make it to the top, where I stopped and waited for her. As she Clambered aboard, I can still see the look of relief and joy on her face, she was so very fond of that old Champ.

Andy my old pal and neighbour told me one day he was coming home from school and met my mum coming from the bottom fields with the horse and cart and a big bag of turnips on her back. She liked a good blether and Andy said, why don't you put the bag down for a wee while and take a breather my mum replied saying "I had a big enough job lifting it up in the first place, If I lay it down I might not be able to pick it up again.

Another time she was helping me unload a trailer full of hay bales when she slipped and slid of the back. Oh no not poor mum again (oh how I loved that woman). I was frightened to look and when I did all the skin on her leg from her knee to her shin was peeled of like a banana skin. I pulled her jersey sleeve stockings back up and reassured her she would be ok. That's the first thing you should do to overcome the shock. I learned that whilst training with the Civil Defense Rescue section. I heaved all the bales off as quickly as I could and sat her on the trailer. I checked the wound, it looked terrible I rolled the skin back up as best as I could, this would save a skin graft I knew, covered her leg with the many rags she wore and rushed her up to Raigmore hospital.

Mum was very well known and quite a character with the A and E team as she had been there not too long before. One of the nurses said you're the lady that was in for a tetanus jab about a fortnight ago so you won't need one this time. I took mum home and she soon recovered her recuperation powers were immense.

Mums visit prior to this involved a cat. We had a lot of cats on the croft, some were quite wild as most of them lived out in the barns to keep the mice and rats down. One of her favourites was a big blue tomcat called Tommy, he was one of old Tigers kittens he was quite a pet, but you could see the wild cat in him. Tommy developed a large cyst on his head and mum and my sister Nan thought it best to take him to the vets out at old Eastgate. Mr. Jolly the vet attended to all our animals. So, mum got dressed threw away her glad rags as she called them and headed to town in Nans car. Mum sitting in the front seat quite chicko as she would say and Tommy on her lap covered with a towel. They made it to Eastgate veterinary and were seen by Ed Jolly who told them to take a seat in the waiting room. A few minutes elapsed and the outside door was suddenly pushed open and in came this man and his dog, of course Tommy didn't like dogs did he and he started to struggle. mum tried to constrain him but he struggled the more and he sunk his teeth right into my poor mums' hand, she shouted in pain and the cat broke free. The door was still ajar and the cat made a bolt for it. He raced across the road, clambered over the wall and onto the railway line and that was the last they saw of poor Tommy. So instead of the cat that needed treatment it was my mum who needed seen to. Mr. Jolly told me to get up to Raigmore and get a tetanus, which she did plus a big bandage.

When Mr. Jolly came to the croft as he did on numerous occasions usually difficult calving, injections etc after my mum died, he often talked about her. I really miss your mother he said, the place is not the same without her, she was a one off. I said well, there's still a few left. No there's not he said, your mum was a unique person. There will never be another like your mum, she had her own special way of doing things, she had her own cats' dogs, hens, cows, calves pet sheep, pet lambs. She had a name for every creature that ever lived on the croft. Mr. Jolly indeed almost everyone got a half dozen free range eggs when they visited.

Mr. Jolly would offer to pay for the eggs saying "are you sure you can afford to give me these ". Mum would say Oh the Lord will provide and sure enough, and I've seen this myself quite often we would find a nest that a hen had hidden with one or maybe two dozen eggs in it.

Ed Jolly used to tell me that my mum believed in fairy's, she used to tell him stories about them. Only certain people can see them seemingly, second sighted people. It's strange but when I think back to my grand aunty Belle who lived at Dunain before us used to say there's fairy's living down at the bottom of the garden, but I never took much notice of her as I was young at the time.

One yarn mum never tired of telling was when we were gathering fruit at her late uncle Duncan's fruit garden. Duncan had a large walled garden at upper Dunain and he grew all manners of fruit Apples, cherries, grapes, strawberries, raspberries, Logan berries, goose berries etc. He sold his fruit to the Moray Firth fruit growers and along with his two cows and calves and a few hens he and his wife Kate had made a good living We lived at Black fold at the time and we used to make our own sandwiches for lunch. Aunty Belle, Uncle Jack and cousin John were up from Blackpool at the time. This day mum was helping grandad to make some tomato sandwiches. Grandad whose eyesight was failing a bit, but he would never admit it was shaking the salt over the sandwiches when the top fell off, there was a mountain of salt on this sandwich and he never noticed slapped the other piece of bread on and gave it to John. My mum could see what was happening but it was too late to do anything. John took one big bite and a couple of chews as he spat it out, there was bits of bread and tomato splattered everywhere. Pooh what salt is on this sandwich said John tears streaming down his cheeks. Grandad could be very firm at times and he said to John, shut up and eat it, you're far too fussy that's what's wrong with you there's people starving in the world and they would be glad of it. My mum could see what distress John was in and she swapped the sandwich for another when grandad wasn't looking.

Uncle Duncan was such a kind lovely man I remember him so well even though I was very young at the time, Aunty Kate was likewise. Such a warm kindhearted woman. They had no family, but they absolutely doted on each other it was darling and dear each time they spoke to each other everyone talked about them and loved them. Aunty Kate took ill and sadly passed away. Poor Duncan was heartbroken inconsolable, he could not live without her and as he had no children to draw comfort from, he sadly took his own life. After a long search they found Duncan drowned in a water reservoir with a bundle of stones tied around his neck, such a sad story, so when Duncan and Kate died my folks took over the running of the gardens for a while.

My mum told me this story about my grand uncle Duncan. she said he was a shy but very brave man who fought in the second world war. He once captured a German machine gun bunker all on his own, He told this story to her with tears in his eyes. He said I crawled up the bunker and got as close as I dare without them seeing me and I hurled a grenade in. It exploded killing all but one a young fair-haired lad. Duncan said he would only be about seventeen clambered out with a luger pistol pointed at Duncan, but he just couldn't pull the trigger. Brushing the tears from his eyes Duncan said I pulled my trigger it was him or me and as the young German lad fell to the ground mortally wounded, he was crying clutching his chest as his life slowly ebbed away. He shouted mamma mamma.

Duncan cradled him in his arms as he watched him slowly slipping away. I don't think that memory ever left him.

One of the most terrifying ghost stories I have ever heard actually on a par with Maggie and Lexy was told to me by a crofter who lived just a few miles away from us at Blackfold. When he told me this story his wife and my late wife Dot were present. Ok snuggle up fold your arms. Oh, and don't forget to close your curtains

I had known Duncan a long, long time since I was a wee boy, maybe five or six years old, which makes this story much more authentic, sadly Duncan is long gone, but Jean his wife is still with us at this time of writing, Right are you still comfy here we go :

When Dunc and Jean got married, they lived with

Jean's folks in town, after a few months Duncan applied for a small cottage to rent.

Which was situated on the edge of the bleak Drumashie moor. his application was successful, and they both moved in. The cottage was mostly furnished which meant they only had to take a few small bits and pieces with them, it was midwinter at the time.

Duncan thought it would be nice to put a wee bit of garden fence around the garden. Jean said that would be nice, I'll start making the supper and I'll give you a shout when its ready. Duncan started digging the post holes, he had quite a large hole to dig for the gate post Duncan stopped for a breather and when he looked up, he found himself surrounded by cats. They were hissing and screeching at him. Duncan was well known for been a hard, fearless man, afraid of nothing, but he said the hairs on the back of his neck were standing up. he tried to shoo them away but most didn't budge. Then Jean shouted him that the supper was ready and to come in as it was getting dark and the snow had started to fall.

Duncan went in and never said a word about the cats, he didn't want to scare Jean. They had their supper and settled in for the night after a blether and a few cups of tea they decided to go upstairs to their bedroom, there were two small bedrooms upstairs.

They weren't long in bed when they heard an unearthly noise, banging and skirling coming from downstairs. Duncan hopped out of bed, crept downstairs and went to the kitchen where this terrible noise was coming from. He tried to open the door, but there was this awful force pushing against him on the other side. With a great effort he managed to push the door open and this cat came bolting through the door with such force it nearly broke his legs. The big kitchen dresser was shaking as if it were going to break into pieces. There were two cats clinging to the top of the dresser, their backs arched, hissing and skirling. When they saw the door open, they made a run for it and shot out.

Then suddenly all was quiet and Duncan tried to make his way back upstairs, but there was this awful force pushing against him, just like when he tried to open the kitchen door. I could see Duncan was feeling really uneasy about reliving all this again (I had heard this story from a third party and now here was Duncan the man who had experienced all this firsthand telling it to Dot and I. I had actually asked him if what I'd heard was true and if he would mind telling me his story. He told me he didn't mind telling me and what he told me was the gospel truth). Duncan said he had to hang on to the handrail and pull himself up the stairs

I'll tell you this folk I wouldn't have stayed another minute longer in that house but Duncan just hopped back into bed and told Jean not to worry it was just the cats fighting.

Duncan wasn't long back in bed when they both heard the front door open and slam shut. They felt a cold shiver running down their spines and next thing this big heavy footsteps coming up the stairs, thump, thump, thump, closer they were coming up then suddenly they stopped outside their door. They both felt a cold evil feeling coming over them. Jean was absolutely terrified, she said "I felt like screaming but I could not let it out something was stifling me. They then saw the doorknob beginning to turn then stop as if it were whatever was outside had gone to the wrong door. Then the footsteps started up again, making their way to the other bedroom thump, thump, thump. They heard the door creak open then slam shut. There was silence for a minute and then Duncan said there was this loud pitched loud curling scream of a woman, as if she was being murdered. As Duncan was telling this story Jean would butt in periodically and say to Dot and I that's true Jim, sure as death I was there, she said, froze in bed absolutely terrified. Then they heard the door creak then again slam shut. Once more they heard those big heavy footsteps coming towards their door. Thump, thump, thump, and then they stopped outside Dunc and Jean's bedroom. Then the footsteps started again, away from the door along the landing and down the stairs, then outside.

Jean by this time was hysterical she was also heavily pregnant. I'm not staying in this house another minute she said to Dunc, I'm leaving. They both Wrapped up with as much warm clothes as they could find and headed out of that awful cottage into the snow. The decided to go to Jeans mums house some seven or eight miles hence. The snow was quite deep by now and they were really struggling, especially Jean, who as I said was heavily pregnant. Then in the distance behind them they saw the lights of an approaching vehicle, it was the county snow plough. They were lucky enough to be seen by the driver as by now it was blowing a blizzard. They were so relieved when they heard the air brakes slamming on and the driver stopped the machine. They clambered aboard into the nice warm cab.

The driver could not believe that anyone would

venture out on a night like this, He said what on earth are you doing out in this blizzard.

Duncan himself, hard tough man that he was, was still trying to come to terms with what he and Jean had just seen and heard. He replied to the driver I can't bring myself to tell you and even if I did, I don't think you would believe me.

As Duncan was telling us this story, he kept looking at me and by the tone of his voice I think he was expecting me to come up with a logical explanation for it all, but how in this world could I possibly do.

Duncan had a brother Jimmy who he met a few days later and he said to Duncan. "What in the blazes made you leave the cottage at Drumashie in yon blizzard if it wasn't for the snow plough you might both have perished ". Duncan told Jimmy as much of the story as he was prepared to listen to and said "What a load of utter rubbish, you wouldn't have got me leaving at that time of night."

Duncan was well fed up with Jimmy's ranting and unbelief and he said to him. OK if you're so brave I'll take you up tonight in the land rover after darkness falls and we'll see if anything happens

So sure enough, Duncan picked Jimmy up in the Land rover and headed for Drumashie moor. They came in sight of the cottage and suddenly they both saw this shape crossing the moor, they described it as this big white ball bouncing on its way towards the cottage and they watched as it disappeared through the gable wall.

I've seen enough said Jimmy trembling, let's get out of here. Duncan said who's so brave now, look at you, you're shaking like a leaf. Needless to say, they spun the land rover around and headed back to town, and in nothing flat they were both clean out of sight of the cottage.

We found out that the cottage was relet to another young couple and they had the same experience. On hearing these events, the local council sent the demolition boys up and raised the old cottage to the ground. You can still see the ruins to this day.

Seemingly the story goes that years before, a crofting couple lived there and one day the husband went to the cattle sale in Inverness to sell one of his stirks. he must have got a good price for the beast as he came home drunk that night, as so many of the old crofters did at that time. He was expecting his poor wife to have his supper ready for him on the table, out by now it was over ready, she had kept it in the oven for him. In a blind fit of drunken rage, he hit his wife a blow on the head with the poker which killed her. I don't know what happened to the man, but I'm sure it will be on the police records somewhere.

(Cliff Westcombe and I) best man at Cliffs wedding

Working on the croft while in my late teens, I used to have to sneak out the door so my dad would not see me. It was ok when he was in the far away fields, but when he was working near the house it was quite difficult to escape.

The tractor was a great thing for dad it was a new toy and he didn't need me as much as he used to, to guide the horse up the drills etc.

My poor mum used to cover up a lot for me, my dad would say to her where's the loon? "He's always skinning off when there's work to be done ". I wasn't supposed to have any kind of social life at all. It was all work and hard work at that. I mean I was lifting one and a quarter hundred weight or so (70kg) when I was twelve years old. I hadn't the nerve to say they were too heavy. That was the weight the bags of lime came in I'd have been better off working in the cotton fields of the deep south, or so I thought.

Where did I skin of to? It was Strathpeffer. THE STRATH, everyone wanted to go there, sometimes three double deckers would leave from Inverness, plus others from Tain and all the surrounds, when I got there it was a magical atmosphere. Not the old accordions, which I loved and still do, but the guitar bands first guitar hand I heard was at the strath Johnny Law and the MI5. Then there was a lot of Irish show bands The Drovers, Larry Cunningham, and more.

Then it was time to visit one of the bars and I always needed a few drams, sometimes more than a few to pluck up the courage to ask a girl to dance. In those days the boys stood in a row on one side and the girls stood in a row opposite.

I thought I was the bee's knees with my John Collier checked suit paid up at ten bob (50p) a week, my fancy embroidered tie with a fake gemstone. Oh, aye and the shoes, canny forget the shoes. Winkle pickers they called them very sharp pointed toes (I'm glad my dad didn't wear them)

I'd been weighing up this girl opposite me for a long time, but every time I picked up the courage to ask her someone would else beat me to it. As the night was wearing on, I thought I would ask her for a dance.

I strode across the ballroom floor (I was more accustomed to striding through a muddy field and made a bee line "more like a butterfly line to this girl who was sitting on one of the chairs lined up against the wall.

I stuttered, could I, I mean would you like, can I have this dance please. She made a move to get up and I couldn't believe my luck. Here was this beauty I had been fancying for a long time and she was going to dance with me, yes little ole me a poor humble crofter. She probably worked in a fashion salon by the look of her.

I threw my fag on the floor real macho style (no ashtrays in those days) and tramped on it to put it out. Gee Wizz I let out a roar of pain. for there was this hole in the sole of my shoe and by Crickey it was hot. I couldn't shake it off in a hurry as it had melted my nylon sock onto my skin which made it worse. The girl suddenly sat down and said no thanks I don't want to dance.

I made a bee line back to the other side where the boys were and I ruefully watched this sod take my girl up for the rest of the dance. I remember that night as if it was yesterday as I had to walk home in my stocking sole. When the sole in our shoe wore thin, we used to or at least I used to cut cardboard insoles and insert them into the shoe to get a few more miles out of them or till we could afford a new pair.

Another night I was at Strath and I ended up on the wrong bus home, it was the bus going to Tain. The complete opposite way to Inverness.

Someone I knew told me and they alerted the Inverness drivers who held the bus up for me until I got on. Gee whizz I didn't fancy walking home from Tain to Inverness in those shoes.

Yet another night, the buses were always full, a lot of people had to stand. I crawled in under the back seat opposite the open door of the double decker bus and fell asleep. You know the kind of sleep I mean when you could almost fall asleep on the top rung of a ladder. I was oblivious to all the singing and blethering that I am sure was going on. The next thing I remember was this banging and thumping on my head. I thought that someone was trying to murder me. Then a torch shone in under the seat and a lady looked on, OH! look there a poor young boy under there. It was the cleaner ladies she had not seen me and she was poking and prodding this mop under the seat and she kept hitting me on the head with it, till she realised that there was someone there. She said to the other cleaner "If it was a young bit of skirt, they wouldn't have left her there. So, they dusted me down. I remember it was snowing and the snow was drifting in the open door. I was covered with snow.

One of the biggest setbacks on the croft was the lack of toilet facilities. It was so embarrassing when people asked where the toilet was and you pointed them to the byre and handed them a copy of the daily newspaper. You had to walk to the byre ankle deep on mud and coo sharn and if it was dark you were in big trouble

Of course, as time wore on, we got an outside chemical loo and dad bought some old chanty pots at a farm sale for under the bed night-time use. Some had no handles, they had been broken off, which was quite handy at times for when it was dark you knew they were full if you got your thumb wet.

Then they had to be emptied we would peek round the end of the house to make sure no one was coming, then run for it, maybe then the postie or someone would come and you would run back inside, splatters everywhere then back outside when the coast was clear. The same procedure taking them back in at night, but at least you had the dark going for you.

One day one of my pals asked me what are those upturned pots lying over there, I told him they were flower pots. He obviously never seen a chanty pot before.

One time I'll never forget was when my dad and I were taking in the corn stooks, I was up on the cart building the load and my dad was forking up the sheaves to me. Once you get up a wee bit, the load can become quite shaky and Sally the horse had a bad habit of taking off without command to get a fresh bite of grass at the edge of the field. She moved this day and took me by surprise. I went over the cart backwards and landed with a thump on my head. I felt a dull thud as I landed and everything went dark and blurred. I heard my dad say out loud, 'Oh the loon, the loon he's fallen off and landed on his head." Thoughts of Andy's grandad must have been flooding through his head as that is how he died, he fell off the back of a load of sheaves and broke his neck.

I was still lying on the ground and dad was kneeling over me. This hard-hard dad of mine was crying "are you alright boy are you alright?" I was too afraid to say no, so I just said I'm ok.

He breathed a deep sigh of relief. When he knew I was OK, his sympathy turned to a wee bit anger," what did I tell you boy, hang on always be ready for a sudden jerk, you know what like the mare is for moving," and with that he hoisted me up on his shoulders and back up onto the load to finish it. the harvest had to be taken in at all costs, well nearly all. I overheard him telling Jock the trapper, shortly after, that he'd got an awful fright when I landed on my head. "I thought we'd lost the loon "he said. So, my poor hard dad was after all very concerned, which shone through his hardness.

Another incident involving the same horse occurred when dad was sowing seed oats in the big top field. It was done by hand, dad had a big broadcast box, which held two full pails, strapped on his back, and I had to keep it supplied with grain, it was a thankless job, trudging over soft fresh ploughed ground with two heavy pails of oats and I was only twelve years old. If I set off too soon, he'd wave his hand and shout, "I'm not ready yet" and if I was a wee bit late, he'd shout "hurry up loon what's keeping you? we haven't all day". As I have said, I had two large tin pails to fill and it was heavy going. One time I was filling a pail off the back of the cart and I left the other one beside the horse, the horse moved again, without warning and somehow ended up with her foot wedged in the pail. The noise of her foot in the pail made her take off and she went thundering up the field cart and all. Clunk, plod, plod, plod, clunk, plod, plod, plod, clunk with me running after her. I think I would have made a good Olympic athlete as I was expected to catch up with the horse, Dad was waving his hands and shouting. Stop her boy or she'll break the cart, but I couldn't catch her and as usual she didn't stop until she reached the end of the field. Her foot was firmly wedged in this pail and I could see the backside of it falling out. Oh, dear I'd get what for now.

After another rollicking, Dad was good at giving me a rollicking he calmed down and said "you better get back to the croft and get another pail and then it was the usual go on boy get of your mark, we haven't all day.

To say that Andy's dad Ian was a legend is a wee bit of an understatement. He was the equivalent of two and a half legends.

One day he went to the sale and he bought a few Irish heifers, they had to be isolated from the rest of the herd until they had passed some veterinary tests. Ian asked me if I could see my way to loan him one of the fields about ¾ of a mile away from his place. Of course, I agreed and he dropped the cattle off at mine.

About two or three days passed and one of the heifers took sick and he had to phone for Jolly the vet. We had both not fully recovered from one of those infamous ceilidhs that's went on at Ian's and when Jolly arrived Ian was still half or three quarters cut. Jolly looked at the beast. Then went to the boot of his car and took out a large can of big tablets. Now turning to Ian, he said I want you to give the cow 24 tablets every six hours. Ian looked at him in bewilderment "twenty-four" aye said Jolly, But the easiest way to do it is to dissolve them in a jug of warm water and give it to her as a drench. Ian was looking at his watch, then at me with that look I'd seen so many times before, he was going to rope me in on this job.

(Andy's brother Duncan and i having a wee jam at Dunain)

(Jamie's first day of school)

It was four o'clock in the afternoon, six hours on and it would be ten o'clock at night, another six hours on and it would be four in the morning.

Ian said to Jolly "don't think I'm walking all the way along here at 10 o'clock at night then 4 in the morning.

Jolly looked at me and winked saying it's a darn sight easier than digging a hole for her. So once again I got roped into helping Ian, we did as the vet told us, how we managed I'll never know, but the cow recovered well after a few days.

Shortly after that Ian had two sick Calves in the byre about two hundred yards from the farmhouse. Mr. Jolly once again was called and he gave Ian some of these large tablets to give to the calves and told Ian to get some bottles of sweetheart stout and some Guinness, very good for sick animals he told us. Ian sent out for the beer and it was delivered midafternoon. After the usual blether Ian said we'd better go and attend to those sick calves. "Frances, Ian's wife told him not to be long as supper was not far off. So, we went up to the byre with the tablets and the carrier bag of beer Ian took the top off one of the bottles took a big swig, then handed it to me. Finish it off he said and I'll open another one for the calves. Well try as we may, the calves would not drink out of the bottle they were looking for a soft warm mother's teat, not a hard glass bottle. Ian would jam the bottle into the side of the calves mouth, but there was more falling on the ground than the calve was drinking.

Temper was rising and Ian said what a flipping waste, he looked at the calves and said, "if you don't drink this we will" and that's exactly what happened we perished the lot ourselves.

We staggered down to the house about an hour later and poor Francis wasn't best pleased "what on earth were you doing up there? Your suppers ruined"

Ach to pot with the supper said Ian as he reached into the cupboard and took out a large bottle of whisky and so we started another ceilidh. Oh, and the calves, they joined in later when we went back up to finish the job.

Blackfold wasn't all ghosts and hard times. A worthy couple of notes, two big robust people Mr. and Mrs. John Lee moved into our old croft house when we flitted to lower Dunain. John was a real highlander, almost, it would seem a left over from Culloden. Never wore English gear as he called it, he was too proud for that. He always wore a kilt, jacket to match, Balmoral and a big pair of the toughest brouges you ever saw. All that was missing was a claymore He was a great piper and excellent at Highland crafts, making sporrans, horn buttons, even skean dubhs.

John, like ourselves loved a good old-fashioned Highland ceilidh and decided to hold one in our old barn next door to his house. There was a good concrete floor in the barn my dad had laid, which was used for threshing the corn sheaves. The rest of it wasn't too bad, there were the odd rotten board and loose sheet or two of corrugated iron. However, John had worked hard getting the place in some sort of order. Hay bales for seats, large tartan rugs, he had probably weaved himself, hanging over the worst cracks in the wooden walls. There was a really good turnout, despite it blowing a real north westerly that night. Nobody was feeling the cold wind especially John who was drinking his favourite drams out of a large horn drinking cup.

During the course of the evening a rather posh but nice woman came over to John and said "Excuse me John can you tell me where you toilet is. "Certainly, Mam piped up John wiping his ginger moustache, come with me. He took the woman by the arm and he opened wide the barn door. The gust of wind that came in, nearly blew the poor woman off her feet. John waived a big hairy arm in all directions. "There you are my dear from here to Lochaber" and with that he spun around and closed the door. I'll bet that that poor woman remembered that episode in her life for a long long time.

The ceilidh went on well into the early hours and John had this wonderful habit of always piping his guests off the premises and this he did till we had all gone home.

John also worked for the forestry commission and the woods were just absolutely infested with midges the great highland midge, the terror of both man and beast, John used to cut big branches of bog myrtle (a bushy moorland shrub) and stuff it up his kilt between his legs to keep the midges away. It must have been a nightmare wearing a kilt when the midges were about.

Bog murtle has a beautiful tangy smell, just walk through it and your clothes have this beautiful unique scent that lingers for days. On a warm summer night, you can smell the sweet scent riding along on the breeze, A large body care company marketed it for a while as a lady perfume, but bog myrtle wasn't a very appealing name, so they called it by its other less familiar name

Sweet Gayle. I don't know what happened to it but it would make an exceptional gent after shave.

One day Dot was reading the local newspaper and she said I see this company Country House Records, are looking for a recording artist, you should apply for that Jim, she said. Oh, I don't think so I said I wouldn't be up for that I'd be much too nervous, Nerves the bane of my life. However, Dot persuaded me to go to the auditions which were being held at Eden court theatre. So, we set off, one Saturday afternoon, there were tents everywhere, people had come from near and far. Of course, when I saw all the people there milling about, I took a severe case of nerves. However, we went into one of the beer tents and Dot and I had a couple of drams and I felt a whole lot more at ease.

Time was wearing on and there was no sign of the auditions starting. They actually had started, but so many people turned up that it was impossible for the record company to hear everyone. So, at last Dot got up out of her chair and said to me I'm going to see what the holdup is. She came back with a not too pleased look on her face. She told me the rest of the auditions were cancelled until a further date.

But Dot was not having any of it. In her own inimitable way, she told the director that her husband had travelled a long way and was not leaving here until they had heard him. Have you ever felt you wished you had stayed at home sometimes. Oh well I was here now and I had another wee dram. We were all ready to go home when one of the directors came over to where we were sitting and said "the management would like to hear you if you could make your way along the foyer and on to the stage. There was a six-piece backing band all ready and several guys sitting in the seats near the front.

The band asked me what I was going to sing, Was it a new song of my own or a standard. I chose Don Gibson "sea of heartbreak "my all-time favourite, so I tuned my guitar into the band and away I went, I was asked to sing another one a slower one I recall and I sang Hank Locklin "please help me I'm fallin". When my audition was over, we shook hands and exchanged contact information and we headed home.

Dot thought I did alright, but I wasn't so sure. I thought I'd heard the last of that, but just a few weeks later a big blue envelope arrived from Country House Records. It read:

Dear Jim, thank you for coming to our auditions on Saturday. We are pleased to tell you that you have passed our audition, but unfortunately, we're not looking for someone at this precise moment but we will keep you in mind

Sincerely yours – Country House Records.

Nobody loved a good Ceilidh better than my old crofter pal Angus Grant He was a tough hardy character as were all the Abriachan and Blackfold people. He was a highly qualified marine engineer, and it was this profession that was the cause of him being involved in a most horrific accident in which he almost lost his life. Where angus was manoevering a big heavy generator it coped over knocking Angus overboard and into the freezing water. He landed on the seabed and the generator fell on top of him pinning him by this leg. He was trapped for a while but the crew managed to free him, bring him to the surface and save his life, but unfortunately, they couldn't save his leg and he had to get an amputation. Poor Angus and he had to return to the croft to make his living.

A good number of years ago Angus bought a large residential caravan to live in as he was renovating his old croft house, badly in need of repair much like our old house at Blackfold. Angus invited all the people that were helping with the renovation and some others to a ceilidh in his caravan and quite a large crowd arrived.

There was a storm brewing that night and the party was in full swing when it started. There were some gusts of wind that would blow you of your feet. His croft was high upon the face of the hill, open to all and sundry. Some of the party goers wanted to leave, but Angus kept feeding them up with drink so that they would stay and most of them did till the break of dawn and by then the gales had subsided. Angus told me after if I had let them go the caravan would have blown away. It was the sheer weight of the people that stopped the gales lifting the caravan and that is why I kept them there said Angus.

Once when we were shearing Angus' Sheep, he took us in for a bite to eat. He went into his cupboard for the frying pan and here was a wee trail of mouse prints in the fat, this wee mouse hopped out from a hole in the wall and Angus batted it over the head with the fish slice. After scraping the pan clean, he fixed us up a hearty meal of sausage, bacon and eggs, never enjoyed a fry up more in my life.

John Logan lived on a croft about a mile away from Angus at the very top of a hill. He had the most magnificent view one could ever wish to see, overlooking the whole of the glen below and Loch Ness, absolutely stunning. John was always known as the boxer. I can't remember why for someone once told me and I have completely forgotten, but he was never a boxer. I remember him well. He was employed by the Highland Council as the road man. He travelled back and fore the road from Abriachan to Blackfold, filling in potholes and cleaning roadside ditches. He was armed with a shovel strapped to his trusty old bike.

The boxer was well known and liked by one and all but he was notorious for his partaking of the crater. He kept a few sheep on his croft, and he was to be seen quite frequently at the local sheep market where he would buy and sell as the case may be.

One day at the sale he bought a nice young ewe to keep up his breeding stock. He had no transport and Abriachan was 15 miles away. He couldn't afford a float especially for one loan sheep. So, John the boxer made his way across town dragging this sheep on the end of an old rope and a short piece of barbed wire. This was all he could find for a lead. It was a strange sight to see the boxer making his way across town with this sheep in tow, heading for his favourite haunt the Gellions bar, the most popular bar in town. He tied the sheep to one of the down pipes on the wall and went into the bar for his evening refreshment.

Closing time soon came around and the boxer thought to himself I'd better hit the trail, the last bus to the trail was leaving town at 10:30. So the boxer bade a fond goodnight to all his old cronies and set off for the bus stop. Dragging the ewe behind him and sometimes the ewe would get in front and drag him along.

I happened to be on the bus that night, it was the old Macbraynes service bus and I well remember it pulling up just out of town as the boxer thumbed it down Dodd the conductor opened the door and asked the boxer where he was going at this time of night. The boxer said I'm going home to the croft. Well said Dodd you can't take that sheep on the bus with all these passengers aboard and then an argument broke loose. Look said the boxer I'll pay for its fare but make it a child's fare I'm a wee bit short of cash. The argument continued to the amusement of all the passengers. Dodd was getting nowhere, and neither was the boxer. Dodd said look here John if the inspector comes on board, I'll get the sack for this. Eventually Dodd gave in and said OK John we'll put the sheep in the luggage compartment, where all the large luggage went. With much huffing and puffing between the two of them they managed to push the reluctant sheep on board and slammed the door shut.

The boxer climbed aboard the bus sat down on the single front seat beside the driver, usually reserved for the conductor but it was Johns for the night and he wasn't shifting. He pulled out a half bottle of whisky from his inside coat pocket and started swigging away as if he hadn't a care in the world and maybe he hadn't.

My bus stop was miles before the boxers so I don't know what happened after that. But one of the local crofters often told me they would be heading down the road leading to the boxers and they would see a large pair of tacketty boots protruding out of the bushes at the edge of the road, and here would be the poor boxer lying fast asleep in the ditch. The Blackfold-Abriachan road had many steep, steep hills to climb and they would tire a fit sober man out. So, I can well understand him stopping for a breather and inadvertently falling asleep.

Taking a good skinful of the old crater on the croft could be a very dangerous thing to do. One crofter I heard my dad say came home one night very drunk and he woke up in the middle of the night with a raging thirst. He picked up a lemonade bottle and took a big swig. In no time at all he was in total agony, someone had put sheep foot rot lotion in the bottle. The foot rot main ingredient was arsenic and some other acids. It burnt a hole in his stomach and he died a horrible death. Shades of Annas parazone bottle at Dochgarroch school. My dad always warned me never to put anything else but drinks in a lemonade bottle.

Times were hard on the croft, very hard, my mum despite her years was very fit and active

Dots five children were at home and I now had two of my own, but we struggled through and they soon grew up. Time and tide wait for no one, Yvonne got a job as a check out girl and helped a bit.

I can't remember what Robbie did but he wasn't used to croft work. He did get some work from a landscape gardening company. Stevie bought a scooter to take him to his work as an apprentice mechanic. Laura led an entangled sort of life, here, there, and everywhere Ah Laura. Sonia well she had a passion for horses and she got a job in a local fruit and veg store.

Laura was a wild one, though, long since cooled down into a very charming individual. Sometimes her mum would ground her but later on when looking into her bedroom you would see the curtains flapping about in the wind. The window wide open and no sign of Laura. then it would be into town scouring all the bars trying to find her. But she usually made her way home.

Sonia managed to get herself a pony. she called him Major and he was a major catastrophe. He was oh so stubborn. Sometimes he would not budge for anyone, especially if there were someone on his back. I remember going to town one day and Sonia was going out for a ride on Major. When I left the croft, Major was digging in and not shifting. Sonia was sat astride, shouting and goading him. I returned home from town and I couldn't believe my eyes, the two of them were still in the same place well not quite I reckon they moved about twenty yards or so. Sonia was still shouting and goading him but to no avail. Ah well that was Major. As time wore on Yvonne, Robbie, Steve, Laura and Sonia all met the loves of their lives and left home. Their exploits would fill another book or maybe more, but I think I'll just leave it for now. I may If time permits put a few tales in later on

So that just left Jamie, Rory, Dot and I at home

It was now becoming quite obvious that I was amassing some debt, my accountant told me that the croft was in a bad way financially and asked me did I not see it coming. I said Well yes but I always thought I would pull out of it somehow.

So, there was nothing else to do but get a job which I got at McDermott's the local oil fabrication yard. This was a soul-destroying job, it involved using heavy air powered grinders to dress up and smooth all the welds. You would have to crawl up narrow pipes, just enough room to squeeze through. Pencil grinders were notorious tools, they were actually banned in Holland and several other countries. The grindings they produced were long razor-sharp needles which stuck into you wherever there was the least gap in your protective gear. With the force of the air power they would get down the back of your neck and inside your boots, Sometime they would manage to get past your goggles and into your eyes, which was serious, you had to go to the yard surgery to get seen to and then to the local hospital where the eye was anesthetized and the grindings extracted. I hated this as it always meant I had to wear an eye patch to prevent further damage and of course I was not allowed to drive and Dot had to come in and take me home. One night I had to have two patches, both eyes were covered. They could be taken off once the anesthetic wore off. One morning Sonia hopped into my bedroom to see if I was OK. She took a fit of laughing when she realised, I wasn't there, but lying on my pillow were these two eye patches, I had already gone to work.

We managed to keep the croft running, but soon I had to part company with some of my cows to pay of some debts. this was a very, very sad time in my life they all had their own names which they knew and they would come to you when called

Polly, Daisy, Rosy, Heather, Morag, Mary, Cherry, Lily and many more

Mum pail fed the young calves and she used to get so attached to them. Each had their own special pail, and they knew when it was feeding time.

It was a very sad day occasion for her when sale day arrived. The cattle float would back up to the byre and mum would edge her way into the house for a good cry to herself. You see these calves were her babies her constant companions throughout her hard life.

When my dad came home from the sale, mum would ask him, who bought the calves but he would never say. Then mum would say with all her country innocence." I hope the butcher never got them" but mostly that's where they went at least the stots (bull calves castrated) did. The heifer calves may have been kept for breeding if they were lucky. Mum would often say to me. It's enough to put you off eating meat seeing all these animals going to the slaughterhouse and I still feel that way even today that is why I so much hate to see beef thrown in the bin. Pure and utter disrespect for the beast that gave his life so that we can live. All parts of an animal should be used and never thrown in the bin.

As Mr. Jolly the vet had once said to me my mum was a one off in her own wonderfully peculiar way. She grew so very attached to her animals. The hens used to follow her everywhere even into the house. One particular pet hen she called Granny because of her age; she laid an egg nearly every day. She would jump up on mum's lap and get petted like a wee kitten. She got a special burial when she died. She's buried in the garden at Blackfold. We had numerous pet lambs. Lambs who were orphaned or their mothers couldn't be bothered with them. Yes, sheep can be very temperamental as well as humans, there's always a Larry amongst them. But this certain year she had the usual Larry and two twins to look after and oh boy did she get so very fond of them. They were Suffolk crosses and they had jet black faces and the characteristics long droopy loopy ears so she called them Loopy and Droopy. It was like something out of a Walt Disney film only real. They were bottle fed with cow's milk. When they were leaving the lamb pen you had to be quick to get the gate shut or they would be out before you could say "Jack Robinson" that was one of my mums favourite expressions. We had several tins in the field for water and oats and other tit bits and quite often you would see Loopy and Droopy with one of these tins jammed on their heads bobbling back and fore as they lay there chewing the cud. That was so funny and even when they got up, they would bang into every obstacle in the field. Sometimes they would accidentally bang into each other. Of course, they seldom came off on their own, we had to catch them to take the tins off. Yes, that was so funny, sort of reminded me of Andy and our school days.

(Mum and a Dutch holiday maker with my old pal Lucky)

(Mum with sick lamb she restored back to health
with Aunty Belle, Blackpool my cousins Alan and
John who grew up to be Procurator Fiscal)

Once we had a lamb badly deformed at birth its legs were all crooked and twisted, it's sort of got along on its front knees and dragged its rear legs. The vet was called out one day to attend a sick cow and he noticed the lamb. He said I couldn't do anything for that, the best thing you can do is put it to sleep. My mum wouldn't hear of it. She persevered with this lamb she called Norman. I remember mum straightening the lamb's front legs every time it went down on its knees and she would stretch them every day, lift the lamb's rear quarters to instill some sort of movement to its legs. She spent many hours with this lamb and lo and behold before long it was running towards her every time it was going to get fed. Sometime later the vet called to see how the sick cow was faring and Norman was prancing about good style. The vet said in disbelief "is that the same lamb which I advised you to put down", mum said "yes". The vet replied "What a credit to you Mrs. Fraser, it's amazing what patience and perseverance can do" and my mum had plenty of both.

We had a lot of cats on the croft to help keep the rats and mice down. We had two with three legs, both as a result of getting stuck in gin traps. One was Fluffy Ann and the other one was called Tootie. My mum had found Tootie as a wee lost and bedraggled kitten wandering about in the lower fields. Goodness knows where she came from, but she soon made her home with us. Some of the cats stayed in the house with us, but most of them were outside in the barn. We had a cat who used to sleep on top of the fire. If my mum had put fresh sticks on it and it was smoldering below, she would lie there till the fire took hold and then jump down when it got too hot. There was an old kitchen range in the croft house at Dunain with a grating and a wee ledge you could place a teapot on. Her fur was all singed at either side, almost to the skin, my father used to say" one day that blinking cat will set the house on fire" and that's what nearly happened. One day we saw her running out of the house with her fur on fire. Thankfully we managed to put it out, When the winter came the poor cat died, she just couldn't stand the cold. She had been so used to the heat all the time.

My sister Nan worked as a domestic in the nearby nursing home Dunain House and she would take home all the scraps in pails. The cats knew the sound of Nan's car as it approached and there was a mass exodus from the house and all the barns. They knew it was suppertime. We had a lovely big white cross Charolais bull which I had bred myself called Charley. My dear mum often told me "nothing ever goes right for you James" she had noticed that very little ever did go right. I had stayed in town with Dot this night, that was before I built the bungalow and as I arrived home in the morning Charley was lying chewing the cud in my neighbour's field. I put on my old clothes and headed down to see what was going on. The march fence was in tatters, broken posts and sagging wires. There had obviously been a fight the night before between Charley and my neighbour's bull. I went over to Charley to get him up and back with his own cows and when he stood up my heart almost stood still, in fact I'm sure it did. Charley's foreleg was hanging limp, it was broken just below the knee. Mr. Jolly the vet came out and examined Charley "look Jim I know what this bull means to you, and I also have watched him growing up from a wee calve to a fine young bull, but it would cost far too much to try and set the bone and he would need to be slung up off his feet for at least a couple of months and it would be nigh impossible". Oh, dear I fought hard to keep back the tears, I didn't want him to see a grown man cry. Although he had seen me breakdown before when he had to put down my dogs. Mr. Jolly said "do you want me to arrange for the slaughter man to come out". I said ok just get it over with. I remember the killer walking over the field to where Charley lay. I watched him from a distance as he took aim almost point blank and I heard the bullet thud deep into Charley's head, that was the end of that ("aye nothing ever goes right for you Jimuck").

My next-door neighbour Houstian or Hugh Fraser was very sympathetic and a good neighbour he was. I couldn't have wished for better. He lent me one of his bulls to take over from Charley so at least I would have calves that season. Then I thought about breeding another bull. One good bull could pay off all my debt if sold at Perth bull sales. So, I went to an auction in Grantown and bought a full pedigree Charolais cow who was heavy in calf, she was called Rosa. This was the dearest beast I ever bought and she would be the last one. Shortly afterwards Rosa presented us with a beautiful bull calf, and we called him Bolero.

Rosa was making a fine job of raising the calf but I noticed even when I bought her that she had one long rear hoof which needed trimming, so I phoned the vet to come out and pare her feet, she was again in calf this time. We put Rosa into the cattle crush my mum and

I assisted the vet. The vet put one rope around Rosa's neck and tied it to the gate post. I held the rear rope which kept Rosa's leg up (I find this very hard to write even after all these years) the vet was almost finished when Rosa went down on her knees. My mum shouted "James, James let the rope go, the cow is choking". The vet shouted "no just hold on for half a minute I'm almost finished" mum was very angry by now "never mind the vet, let the rope go she's choking". The rope around her neck was tight as tight could be, her whole weight was on it and she would have weighed almost a ton. Rosa was a big, big animal. I undid the knot and to my utter sheer and utter disbelief I felt her go limp, her neck was broken. My poor mum was so upset, she had witnessed so many sad and tragic events on the croft, she was crying not just for the cow but for me "how much more of this could poor James take" she told the vet. "I knew that was going to happen" mum said "but you wouldn't listen" poor mum was usually always right. And so, ended another sad chapter in my life on the croft. Now this tragedy meant I had to rear Bolero on my own. There is no real substitute for mothers' milk and now I had to buy expensive bull feed and by gosh they were expensive. Nuts, meal oil cake vitamins and minerals all mixed together to make a highly nutritional but hugely expensive diet. I had to round up Bolero twice each day, put him in a small pen I had made and give him his feed. It took him long enough for him to acquire a taste for the mixture, he much preferred the lush green grass, but he wouldn't get up to a proper weight on grass alone, so the mix was a must. Eventually he got used to it, but he was getting quite hard to handle.

I did manage to get Bolero halter trained and he was getting quite used to it although I had to watch I was always near a fence so I could make an escape if I had to. One day I had him out for a bit of exercise and to my horror I looked down and somehow the halter had slipped over his head and onto the ground. I managed to give the rope a quick sharp tug and it was up around his head where it should have been.

Things by now were getting way out of hand, I had borrowed so much to complete the bungalow, and as the bank manager said "half a house is not much security, just go ahead and finish it off". That was all good and well but now they were wanting their money back. This was turning out to be a nightmare, worse in fact because when you wake up from a nightmare everything's ok, but when I awoke every morning all my worries were still there in fact, they seemed to have worsened day by day. I had to sell my cattle, yes, all my cows and calves and poor Bolero he had to go as well, he grew to be very friendly with me over the past few months. When the cattle went into the ring at auction, they kept turning around looking at me as much as to say, what are you doing getting rid of us, we don't want to go. I felt so sad and so bitter this was definitely one of the worst days of my life. If cows could only speak.

My wife Dot was doing her bit working in two hotels part-time to try and make ends meet, but it wasn't enough what actually kept us going and kept the banks of our backs was the promise of the sale of building plot which would have taken us right out of the bit. The big hold up was the lack of a water supply. We were promised many years back the council would put in a mains water supply, but every time I enquired about it, I was told "it's been put back until next year, but you will definitely get a supply" this went on month after month year after year, We have left the croft now some thirty years ago and there's still no water mains supply to the croft. At last, the bank lost patience, my lawyer said to me "you're a bit of a cause celebre with them, it's come to the point that they're not believing you about the building plot". I sold some fields for a meagre price in trying to keep the house.

I never told Dot this at the time, but my lawyer told me that the bank had obtained an eviction order and the bailiffs were coming to evict us on Christmas day. That was the worst Christmas day of my life. Every minute that passed I was waiting for a knock on the door. Actually, my lawyer had pleaded with them to show some Christmas spirit and it obviously prevailed as the knock never came. So, at last the house had to go and it broke my mum's heart when we told her we were leaving. All the hard-back breaking work she had put into the croft now counted for nothing. Nothing but memories and the place was full of them. It was there she played as a wee lassie her and her dog Crouger and enjoyed so much time with her aunty Belle. What hit me really hard was poor Jamie my son, it was his inheritance and now it would be taken away from him, but there was no other solution apart from a win on the lottery. I still feel very bitter about that, but as always mum said "the Lord will provide and I'm sure he will". I have somehow come to terms with it now and my mum understood the situation better than I, she knew I didn't want to leave Dunain but she said "you couldn't keep on going the way you were doing". I was never cut out to be a towny, I was a real country yokel. The rest of Dot's family had all gone their own ways by now. "It's a sad day we left the croft" is often joked about, but I don't want to go through anything like that ever again. Dot and my mum threw theirs arms around each other and they cried and cried and cried. I think I was more shocked than anyone, was this really happening. All my life I had worked the ground it was in my blood, my very bones. Nothing smells nicer than fresh turned earth behind the plough, or fresh hay, curing in the stacks. The unique smell of a newborn calf or a newborn lamb, but alas it was really happening to me and I had to face up to it. Dot had managed to get a small, terraced house in town so we settled in there as best we could.

I was still working at McDermott's oil fabrication yard at this time and I'd pay a visit to my mum when I could. It seemed so strange going down the old road to the croft. There lying in the bushes at the side of the road was the old pram Rory used to push back and fore up to his grannies for his porridge. Looking down at the lovely new bungalow I built for Dot and all the children, not for anybody else. Seeing strangers in the garden, a strange dog barking at the door it just didn't seem right, but that's the way it was.

Next thing to happen was the last big order at McDermott's was nearing completion and the payoffs were starting and soon it was my turn to go. McDermott's were paying really good money and I was slowly getting back on my feet, but now I had no job. Company's, bosses were not keen to hire ex McDermott's workers as they knew that if McDermott's got another order, they would all go back to them. Now the going got tough again and we sold up and managed to get a rented house in the country. A good friend of mine just happened to be personnel officer with a large manpower company, and he said the best place to go would be Belfast, Harland, and Wolfe who built the Titanic were recruiting and the men needed accommodation. The plan was (and it was a good plan) to rent houses and then re-let rooms to the workmen. This was proving to be a really good earner, but the troubles were still going on and one had to be careful where you went and what you did, you might inadvertently step on someone's toes, who was already at the re-let business and I didn't fancy a kneecapping. You were always under a lot of suspicion, but as usual with my laid back friendly Scottish accent, they accepted me and gave me a lot of advice on how to stay out of trouble. Of course, there was lots of places you just didn't go, if you trod on someone else's patch there would be a knock on your door and asking for a cut of your takings which you would have to pay over or else.

I thought it was so funny some places didn't pay electric or utility bills the meter readers were too afraid to enter the street let alone the houses.

George and I passed a couple of men gagged and tied sitting on a bench beside the motorway and George say's "that's two-meter readers, that's what they do to them".

George my friend who set this wee business up moved me into his old house and said "ok Jim you're on your own now," but he gave me two really good contacts in case I ran in to trouble. I wasn't in the house more than half an hour and the doorbell rang and there standing on the doorstep was my first visitor the TV licence man. He'd obviously been watching from across the street. He'd plucked up the courage to come to the door, so I had no option but to get myself a license.

I was on my own at this time and the houses were doing ok so we thought it best if Dot and Rory and the two dogs came over. Jamie had a good Job with the Royal Mail so he decided to stay with his stepsister Yvonne. Times were still pretty hard and there was always a shortage of spondulucks (money).

One day Dot, Rory and I went to Newtonards a wee town just down the road from Belfast. Dot and Rory went into this shop leaving me standing outside with my usual sorrowful face. Dot's sister Laura once said at a funeral "hey that's a job that would suit Jim, driving the hearse he's got such a sad sorrowful face". Gee I didn't think I was that bad, however here's me standing outside this shop, goodness knows what Dot was doing, probably having a cup of tea and a pie, she always used to tell people "oh Jim never eats through the day anyway". I looked up and there was this trampy mannie on the other side of the road waiting to cross and then he made a beeline straight for me. These guys seem to know suckers when they see one. I've been tapped many a time in Inverness. He come up to me, he seemed nice amicable character he had an old black battered trilby hat on with a feather stuck in it and clothes to match. (Dot would say that the tramp mannie was smarter than me) Before he could open his mouth, well almost, he was about to speak. I said to him I know you were going to ask me for a few bob, but I'm really down on my luck, I'm absolutely skint. "Oh dear" said the trampy "sure have you got nothing at all at all". I said not a brass farthing and I spun him my tale of woe, what sadness, what sorrow and the poor trampy broke down in tears at my story. He threw his arms around me and said "I haven't got much but I can give you the price of a cup of tea and a biscuit" I thanked him, but said no. We exchanged a yarn or two and we bade farewell to each other, he was still in tears when he left. I was a wee bit upset myself., Then Dot came out of the shop wiping some tomato ketchup from her lips and she said "what's wrong with you" I told her about the trampy she said "I know I saw you talking to him, trust you taking money of a poor wee trampy" I said I didn't take money of a poor mans and anyway he was probably better off than I was and anyway he had a better pair of shoes than I had.

Shoes oh aye shoes, sore subject they keep cropping up everywhere. The shoes I had on that day were a bit worn to say the least, but they were comfy. I got them in a charity shop, I wore them a lot when I got home, they had their own air-cooling system, a hole in the toe and a hole in the heel. The souls were flapping about like a pair of walrus flippers, I kept them for slip ons about the house. One day my daughter Sonia wanted to come along with me to Tesco's for some messages, as we wandered round the store, Sonia said why is everyone staring at your feet. She looked down and she said "Jim you're wearing those old bachles of shoes, I had genuinely forgot to change them. Sonia said "that's awful I'll pretend I'm not with you" and she walked away, we still talked about it even today. I always had a thing about shoes, people would ask me "what size of shoes do you take?" I always said 8 ½ upwards because I knew that if someone had a pair of size tens they would most likely say "oh they won't fit you" or "you could have them but with two or three pairs of socks they would be alright".

As the croft was now sold, just the old house and some buildings remained where my sister and my mum lived. My sister Nan managed to build a new house on the site of the old one, this would make my mum's life so much easier. In the old house there was no heating whatsoever until you got the old open fire lit and it took ages to warm up. It was absolutely Baltic in the winter especially first thing in the morning, it took some effort to get out of bed. The new house was a great boon to mum, after all those years of hardship especially the harsh unforgiving winter of Blackfold, she now had central heating, hot and cold water a proper toilet and bathroom but through it all I'll bet she wished that I was still there with her living in the old but and ben. Then one day I received some dreadful news. Nan came to tell me that mum had gangrene in her big toe and they were planning to amputate just below the knee. The doctors didn't tell mum at first, they said they would do what they could to save her leg. When I visited mum in hospital that night, she said "Jimuck what will they do to me, be honest with me now, I'd rather know" I didn't beat around the bush I said look mum they may have to take your leg off. Oh, dear did I really say that there was no one I loved more dearly in the whole wide world than my mum, I wanted her to be prepared for the surgeon's decision to amputate. She brushed a tear from her hazy blue eyes and she thanked me for being honest with her. "At least now I feel a wee bitty better, knowing". So, it came to pass, the surgeons tried all they could in their powers to save mums leg but alas to no avail and the dreaded day arrived for her operation. The operation went well but it was a huge shock to a lady as fit and active as my mum. The doctors tried to fit her with an artificial leg but it hurt her too much she said, so it was wheelchair bound for my poor mum now. I looked at her stuck in this horrible contraption of a wheelchair and vivid memories of the past came flooding through my mind. Memories of oh so sweet days gone by. Working side by side, making hay ricks in balmy late summer days, lifting stones off the ploughed fields, lifting tatties and clipping swedes in cold winter conditions. All these were gone now drifted away as the mists that creep slowly over the hills, gone but never forgotten. My sister Nan nursed my mum for the rest of her years in their new house at Dunain, she took her in the car everywhere, mum loved her jaunts and visits. I will be forever grateful as long as I lived to Nan for what she did for mum. She wouldn't hear of mum going into a home. Wherever mum went she seemed to be a celebrity. She kept everyone at the Mackenzie centre engrossed with her stories and beautiful Highland demeanor. She was always priority with the doctors and nurses when she had to go to hospital for her regular check-ups. This used to embarrass mum as she always said "there's a lot more people worse off than me and in need of more attention" she hated been a burden on people. I was in Belfast with Dot and Rory when I got a call from Nan telling me mum had taken ill. She had to be admitted to the Royal Infirmary with a bad sickness bug, mum was now 85 years old and her resistance to bugs would be much less than when she was younger. I find this next part of my story very hard to tell, my eyes seem to be welling up all the time, so I headed back across the Irish sea to Inverness and be reunited with my mum, just to see that lovely innocent welcoming smile always accompanied with a little tear. She was very ill but she had all her faculties about her and I stayed a couple of days. I thought it best if I went back to Belfast as I had some pressing business there; make sure the two dogs were ok and then come back to stay with mum, for however long.

So, I told mum I would have to go back to Ireland, but I would be straight back. Then she said something that really broke my heart, she sat up in bed and said "I wish I was going with you Jimuck" as she called me "take me with you" she reached out and clasped my hand. I could feel her warm but now wizened hand in mine, fingers twisted with arthritis from years of hard work, but it felt so good. I'm sorry mum I'd love to but I can't take you and then I started trying to explain about the croft "Mum, I said I had no option but to sell the croft "oh yes" she said "I knew all what you were going through and I know you did your best, but it wasn't to be". We bade each other a very fond farewell and I headed back to Belfast. Next day I got a phone call that mum was failing. This oh so tough woman who I thought old father time had forgotten about. I had visions as many other people had of my mum living to be a centenarian. So, I got things in order and caught the next ferry back to Scotland. I rushed to the infirmary door and there I met a friend waiting for me. He said "I think you're just a wee bit too late". I said to myself, that can't be mum has always waited for me, throughout all my life she always waited for me. I rushed into the ward to be at her side. My sister Nan was sitting at the foot of the bed. Providence had reserved my mums bed side for me. I grasped her hand which was still lovely and warm. One of the two nurses told me she was gone, but the other nurse said "no, she knew you would be back, she waited for you, she kept asking us will James be long". Mum was still with me when I sat at her bedside for her eyes opened ever so slightly as she took one last fond look at her son. Then she was gone, she had waited for me after all, oh dear could I go through all that again, I don't think so. I was truly blessed having a mother so special so very special and I thank the Lord to this day. The strange thing was just like her uncle John Blackfold had done all those many moons ago. Mum called all the nurses around her and thanked them for their care and kindness. Then my mum said "this is not the end; this is only the beginning I can feel I am in the presence of the Lord". Now where could one find or hear more comforting words than these. I felt a great burden being lifted of my shoulders; I don't think I could have coped otherwise. I know where my mum is and that is where she always wanted to be.

Now there is a little country churchyard just out of town on the Loch Ness road at Bona, and that's where my mum now lies beside her husband my dad Alexander and their infant daughter Isobel Anne. It is so quiet and peaceful a lot of our kin are buried there. There are two magnificent yew trees which sway in the wind like two giant guardians, watching over the graves. My dad was sextant there for most of his life and many a time he and my mum and I cut the grass. Dad would scythe the bulk of the grass and mum and I would trim around the gravestones with the sheep shears. Now at last that was all over for them, their toil was finished. "Home at Last". As for me I packed up my few belongings and my sorrows and headed back to Belfast. I was really wanting to come home by this time. Opportunities had all evaporated. Harland and Wolf had no more orders to fulfil so there were no workmen to fill our houses, but we had nowhere to go, no place to call home. One day my sister Nan phoned and told us that there may be a cottage on the Dochfour estate coming up for rent. So, Dot headed back to Inverness and her and Nan went to enquire about it. I thought to myself slim chance, very slim chance. Dot phoned later that evening and to my surprise she said "we've got the cottage if you still want it". Want it, oh boy did I want it, this was our only chance of returning back home, back to my roots the place where I went to school and grew up in. Rory was never happy in Belfast anyway and he was absolutely plagued with eczema and hay fever on top of this severe learning difficulties. I am and will be forever most grateful to the landlords of the cottage, The Right Hon Alexander and Gina Baillie for giving Dot and I this chance. So, I cheerfully headed back to Inverness for a hire van and then back to Belfast. We packed everything in, what a tight squeeze it was and I left a corner at the back for which to smuggle our two dogs over. Then we set sail for bonnie Scotland and home to our new abode at Dochgarroch just outside Inverness on the magnificent Dochfour Estate. The cottage was more than ideal more than I'd expected, although I remember them being built when I was a wee boy of about 9 years of age.

There was a tall garden fence all around ideal for keeping our two dogs Lassie and Sasha in. There is a good size garden at the front and a much larger one at the rear. Dot absolutely loved gardening and every chance she got you would know where to find her. Every time she would come home from town, she would have pots and plants which she used to hide under the garden bench so as I would not see them, I was kept busy cutting the grass in our garden and all the outside driveways surrounding the cottage, I also cut the lawn at the restaurant next door, I quite enjoy this as it is good exercise for me. I try to keep the whole place as tidy as I can as I know our landlord likes it that way as the estate is kept in a beautiful condition, and that's the way it should be. Taking a pride in your place and surroundings. My youngest son Rory was born 3rd January 1980 and not long after birth we realised that all was not well with him, he was showing signs of severe learning difficulties. Rory started to take fits, one day he took six fits in quick succession, I thought we had lost him, I told Dot just keep him breathing till the ambulance arrived. He was rushed to hospital where they managed to stabilize him and they put him on pheno barbitone tablets. He got over his fits apart from a very odd occasion. Rory had to attend a school for children with special needs, but I often wondered if he would have been as well attending a mainstream school. Then this horrible nightmare started, Rory was suffering from eczema, really bad. His scalp and body, legs and feet were all affected, by this scourge of all diseases. When he was young, he used to call me Jim. I think Jamie got him out of the habit and he started calling me dad. Rory would lean over the edge of the bath and with tears in his eyes he would say "help me Jim, please help me". Whilst in Belfast it started to get much worse. He would start crying in the early hours and i would take him up to the outpatients, but they were helpless as i was. They gave him the usual useless creams and steroids which had to be used sparingly due their potency. It was terrible to watch every night and early morning; we would hear him crying. I would get up put on his creams and the Belfast hospital told us to put on wet and dry bandages an absolute nightmare. This would settle Rory for half an hour or so then we would hear the oh so familiar crying and moaning I'd go upstairs and all Rory's bandages would be lying in a heap on the floor all except one, which he always chewed till it was in shreds.

I had heard that alternative medicine and Chinese medicine were curing or at least helping a lot of people, it became obvious by now that mainstream medicine had no answer to this eczema problem. It just so happened that there was a Chinese practice on the Lismore road just a mile or two from where we stayed. I'll never forget the lady doctor, Dr Gui she examined Rory and prescribed herbs, but she said "you might have a bit of a job getting Rory to take them, if at all".

Seven bags of herbs consisting of; twigs, bark seeds, leaves and grass. Dr Gui told us to boil them in a non-metallic pot, cooled and then drank in two equal servings. Oh, dear what a stink when they were boiling. Dot said "how on earth do you expect anyone to drink that", but Rory wasn't just anyone. I filled a three-quarter tumbler with the potion to our amazement he drank it in one great gulp. After just two days of this i noticed Rory had stopped scratching, there was no sign of the big, long crack in the skin at the back of his neck which had been causing him great bother in moving his head. The improvement was remarkable, but alas at £5 per bag seven bags a week we found it impossible to keep up the treatment so the eczema returned after two or three weeks of complete relief and Rory was referred to the skin specialist at the Royal Ulster hospital. We told him about the Chinese treatment and he got quite angry, "stop that treatment right away, it's dangerous and herbs are poisonous". Then i said to him Well what can you do. "Look" said the specialist "very little" we don't know, nobody knows the root cause of eczema. He prescribed more creams and little blue pills which I found out later almost killed Rory. They had to be given for a short time only or risk serious complications if continued. They cleared up the eczema, a quick fix but it came back worse than ever. The district nurse with all her experience told me that this would happen. So, we were really back to stage one. I was still hoping to get Rory back on the Chinese medicine but then we returned to Inverness and I thought that had ended all hope of that. On returning back home to Inverness I discovered that there was an alternative medicine practice run by a Dr Kassim in town. I went to visit him and much to my surprise he said "yes, i can cure Rory, take him in to see me". This we did, but the doctors herbs were in tincture form 5ml one teaspoon taken in hot water, much easier for Rory and much cheaper at twelve pounds for three weeks treatment, than the bagged herbs. After a short while the eczema cleared up apart from the odd flare up. After a year or so the eczema started to get bad again, years of pain, sleepless nights followed for all of us. Bandages on arms and legs, neck and sometimes body stockings which were really difficult to put on. I would dress him give him his drinks and in no time at all, I would hear Rory crying again and find all the bandages lying on the floor. I had to do the same procedure all over again. Dot helped when she could, but Rory usually insisted that i put his bandages on as I had a knack of putting them on with all the practice I had. But now I started to take things into my own hands and I did a lot and I mean a lot of research realising the futility of modern medicine.

I heard of and got in touch with an American lady Lesley Taylor who was diagnosed as terminal with just a few months to live. She travelled to the Amazon rain forests and lived with the Indian tribe there and she quickly learnt a lot about all the amazing rain forest herbs and their healing powers. She quickly found a recipe which included a wonderful herb called "cats' claw" and several other herbs which she brewed up and started taking and she began to get better. On her next visit to her oncologist, he broke the news to her that she was almost completely cancer free. She told him of the "cats' claw" and the other herbs, but he refused to believe that the herbs had anything to do with her miraculous recovery and said that it was the chemo and radiotherapy that was the reason for her recovery. This was after she was told there was no more, they could do for her, it was the chemo and radiation that nearly killed her. She had a very successful business which she gave up and ploughed everything into the new Rainforest Herbs Project, which was just as successful.

Then she printed her amazing book, probably the best book I ever bought a remedy for every disease under the sun. I never was an advocate for the EEC or the European Union as it was once called and one of the main reasons is explained here. The author of this book sold all her herbs mostly in capsule form and they helped thousands of people, with cancer, eczema, lupus etc, but then the EEC proposed a ban and were successful in prohibiting the sale of these herbs, their claim being that the herbs were dangerous. There are dangerous herbs out there but the herb companies are well aware of these and they stay well clear of them. The drug companies had a lot to do with this i suspect. All that money they receive just wasted on useless drugs that do more damage that the disease itself. We hear about this great new drug but it won't be available for another five years or so. I am now 74 years old and I've been hearing about this cure just around the corner all the time. Cancer is at an epidemic rate at the moment, I've lost so many relations, friends and neighbours to this disease. So, this lady gave up her business and one can no longer buy these wonderful herbs she sold. One is not allowed to make any claims on what these herbs can do. My own Chinese doctor in town had to clear all her shelves of her capsules. They can't stop you buying herbs in loose form as you can class them as for brewing teas. This is what i now do for Rory. I buy empty capsules and stuff them with the various herb powders. Although

Rory could be prone to a flare up now and then his condition is 95% better than it was years ago.

I have two formulas which i give to Rory but make no claim about them. Rootbark of the peony tree/ Japanese honeysuckle/ peppermint/ atractylodes root/ bark of the amur cork tree/ sophera flaverence, all in capsule form.

Sarsapararilla/ Neem/ Burdoch Root/ Coriander/ Gotu Kola. I put these into a large teabag and bag and boil for 20 minutes or less.

One herb that just possibly could not do without is "cats' claws". I was plagued from my youth up with a serious back problem, oh not a good old fashioned back ache. But pain resulting from my left leg being pulled out of its socket when i was in my early teens. I couldn't straighten up after bending without being in terrible pain. Splitting logs, picking tatties, cutting grass, weeding and so on. Since using cats' claw i just don't, get sore backs any more what a blessing. These herbs were put on the earth by our creator for our benefit (genesis 1;29 and God said behold i have given you every herb bearing seed which is upon the face of all the earth, and every tree, in the which is the fruit of a tree yielding seed, to you it shall be for meat)

Rory's great passion is a boat called the Jacobite Queen. One of a fleet run by Loch ness by Jacobite. He eats and drinks Jacobite Queen.

You're not allowed to call his favourite boat

Queen: he'll quickly prompt you and say it's the Jacobite Queen. Since we came home from Belfast, every night after supper he would take the camera and we had to go in to where the Jacobite Queen was moored at Tomnahurich Bridge just to see it was all in order ship shape and Bristol fashion, Rory tells everyone he is looking after the boat for Freda the owner who he absolutely adores. He would check all the ropes were tied correctly and that the ramp was in position. You can get a good conversation going with Rory, he is quite bright in fact very bright. His spelling is immaculate despite his learning difficulties but he really shocked me one night, it was after supper and we set out on the usual nightly pilgrimage to see if the Jacobite Queen was ok. When we pulled into the bridge i said to myself oh no, there were about a dozen or so kids diving off the top deck. I knew he wouldn't be best pleased, but what he did next shocked me. I'd never seen this side of him before. He threw open the car door and said "right you lot get off that boat, you're not allowed onto it without Freda's permission". He started ushering them off, but a couple of diehards who Rory actually knew refused to go. I was waiting for a barrage of abuse from them and i was quite unsure how to handle the situation. One has to be careful how you treat kids nowadays not like in my younger days where you were likely to get a skelp on the lug or a good old-fashioned foot on the backside. However, Rory stood his ground and he kept telling them to shift or he would physically put them off himself. Eventually they all left and was i glad. That was what the conversation was all about for days after. I've lost count of the number of photos I've taken of the Jacobite Queen every time it gets its new coat of paint and sometimes in-between, he wants a new photo taken of her. There has not got to be a trace of another boat in the photo, which can be quite difficult if there are boats nearby. Even a car or a person in view, warrants another photo. I've lost track of the number of T-shirts he's got with the Jacobite Queen printed on the front. Loch Ness by Jacobite has really expanded into a five-star business. They have four beautiful boats or ships i suppose, so now Rory has the whole four of them printed on his T-shirt. He is so proud of them; he shows them to everyone who shows even the slightest interest. Then one day news was going around the village that Jacobite were interested in having their headquarters shifted to the old estate office and you wouldn't guess where this office might be. Well, it just happened to be right next door to our house. Rory was by now mega excited Loch Ness by Jacobite are really extending their business just outside our home at Dochgarroch. New piers for the boats, a large extension to the existing village hall, for shop, restaurant etc.

PROFILE: Mrs Jessie-Ann Fraser

As the eldest of three children Mrs Jessie-Ann Fraser was born on the 21st of April 1914. Her family has lived in the area for more than five generations and she herself has lived here for most of her life.

She was born on the family croft at Blackfold and has fond memories of her time in the hills catching, rabbits and 'pitting' turnips, which made up part of the family's staple diet at that time. She also remembers delivering a daily flagon of milk to Miss Cameron of Locheil at Dunain House when she was seven years old.

After leaving school at the age of fourteen she secured her first job as a housemaid for General and Mrs MacFarlane at Dunain Park. During her stay there she enjoyed being treated as one of the family, and clearly remembers having the General in the dining-room each morning for prayers before the start of the working day. The General also took her and the other staff at Dunain Park to services at Inverness Cathedral every Sunday. At the age of seventeen Jessie-Ann decided it was time to move on and she went to work at the 100 room Pitmain House shooting lodge in Kingussie. It was there that she met her life long friend May Spencer - they still keep in touch today - who told her about the bright lights of London. Undaunted, Jessie-Ann decided to take the plunge and asked for the help Jean (Rev Pennell (the then minister at Inverness Cathedral and later bishop at Dornblane.) He put her in touch with a wealthy London based toy planting family who, because of her excellent references, were glad to offer Jessie-Ann a post.

The big city had many surprises for a Highland lass like Jessie-Ann. Coming from an area where people didn't even bother to lock their doors at nights, she

Jessie-Ann Fraser during her stay in London in 1936.

had to learn fast. However, being in London at the time of that other Royal crisis, involving Mrs Simpson, was exciting for her. Jessie-Ann also tells an amusing tale of when she saw a 'baldheaded tramp' sitting on the pavement of a London street. She later found out that this 'tramp' was in fact Ghandi, the famous leader over for a visit from India.

A later short holiday break back home at Blackfold turned out to be the permanent arrangement for Jessie-Ann. Her uncle John Shaw had fallen ill and she was needed to help run the family croft. She then married neighbouring crofter Alexander Fraser in . They inherited the 21 acre croft and settled down to a hard life running it. As well as running the croft they made ends meet by working for Docsfour Estate where her husband was a gardener. They then had a second lucky break when they inherited the croft at Lower Dunain. Crofting laws at that time meant couldn't own two crofts so they were forced to sell the croft at Blackfold. Today, Jessie-Ann lives in her comfortable bungalow on her croft at Lower Dunain.

Suggestions for this page should be sent to the editor.

All this going on right next door to Rory's house. I couldn't believe it. Coming all the way from Belfast to live right beside Rory's special interest. Before the Jacobite Queen, his great interest was touring buses parked at Eden court theatre. That was another nightly routine, i don't know how i am still sane. But now the Jacobite has taken a huge weight off my shoulders Rory can be very demanding and with his learning disabilities i find myself maybe doing too much for him, but anything for a quiet life. I have to laugh and so do my friends and family. When I tell them, what Rory said and still says to me. I say to Rory "I don't know what you'll do when I'm not here" he catches me by the lapels and says "look here you're going nowhere boy, you'll always be here". He gets right annoyed when i say that to him, oh well maybe I will always be here like the wandering Jew.

(Dot and I)

My wife Dot was very ill just prior to this and I found myself having to look after her quite a lot.

Her breathing was bad and she had been on hard drugs for her rheumatoid arthritis which involves very frequent tests. Dot was losing weight pretty fast and she was not eating much at all, but the doctors said there was nothing wrong, all her scan and tests were clear. It was only too obvious that there was something very seriously wrong. Dot was on seven different drugs, one being this horrible methotrexate for which she was closely monitored every two or three weeks for serious side effects. Sometimes I'd come home and she would be sitting on the side of the bed with her back to me using an inhaler, she didn't want me to know she was using one. Poor Dot, i did know but i never let on to her. Dot had stopped smoking for a good number of years but she had developed COPD and was having serious problems with her breathing. Dot was never away from the doctor, sometimes she would come home and i would say "gosh you weren't long today" "oh, Jim" she would say "my appointment is not until tomorrow" she was now down to about eight stone and this day she came back from the doctors waving a little pamphlet "how to take care of a person with cancer" that said it all and it was stage four, terminal. I never felt so numb in my life, but I had to face up to it and i was going to be there right beside her all the way. I had my mind made up.

Seemingly there was a tumor between her lungs and they could not operate. She went through the usual radiation therapy but by now her appetite was non-existent. Now it was back to the drawing board for me and I managed to start getting her appetite back, with a wonderful product " ceregumil" and some herbs, which included pure 95% curcumin. I made her little pans of barley broth every day, she really enjoyed that and sometimes she said "i fancy a fish" and i would go to the chippie and take her home a lovely big piece of haddock. She said not to bother, but you know folks I would have climbed to the top of mount Everest for a fish for her. But it was now the shortage of breath that was most worrying, every night when she would lie down it got worse, I would get up and nurse her with menthol crystals in a vaporiser. This went on for a few months. Every night it was terrible to watch i felt so helpless. One really bad night I had to phone the emergency services and the paramedics came out with a nebuliser. Oh, she started smiling and told them that this was a great relief, but unfortunately, they could not leave it with her as they had not got a spare one. Dot got over the bad turn and she was a deal better for a while and she used to tell everyone "I couldn't get over this without Jim, no way" this made me feel a lot better within myself but the huge regret I had and still have about not getting her over it, still haunts me. After a while the breathing got really bad again. The emphasis was now away from the cancer and on the COPD.

We were going to buy a nebuliser, but Julie the Macmillan nurse said to me "I'll get one tomorrow". Julie was a brilliant lassie well cut out for her job, however next morning Dot took really bad, she was shouting for me to get an ambulance, she could not breath she was fighting for her life now. The ambulance came and i just got that feeling that Dot would not be coming back. These big blue eyes staring at me as she sat strapped in the ambulance chair. I followed the ambulance in and at Raigmore the doctors came into the room to see me and just told me quite casually that Dot was not going to make it. Then he said "would you like to see her; we've got her stabilised now" I went in and she didn't look like a woman who was about to die. She was thin certainly, but strong. She was drugged up with i don't know what through a tube in her arm, she kept sitting up and hugging me telling me she was afraid oh, it was heart-breaking. Then she whispered in my ear several times" when am I going to get my operation Jim" poor Dot thought they were drugging her in preparation for an operation. That almost split me in two, we had been through so much together, half of which i have not told in this book and here it was about to end. One of us would be left alone and that one was me. I left late afternoon to attend to Rory to get his herbs and drinks and I left her there with her daughter Yvonne and sister Laura who had stayed all night with her. I wasn't home long and the phone rang, telling me to come in at once but to drive careful. When I arrived, Dot was gone and i can't add any more to this episode in my life, Julie arrived the next day with a nebuliser, just a day too late she could not believe Dot had gone so quick.

This was a really bad time in my life. A friend of mine came to the door and told me that my sister Nan who lived in town was seen out wandering at all hours of the night. So, I had to arrange for carers to come in and I paid daily visits to make sure she had food in the house, she was throwing a lot of good food out. This was the start of dementia. Then I was diagnosed with skin cancer and I had to have several plastic surgery operations on the head. I've got a part of my arm and a part of my neck implanted on my head. I had been putting this off for a while but the lesions were getting too big to be put off any longer. Then I underwent an operation on one hand for carpal tunnel and I postponed another operation on the other hand as I had it treated with acupuncture by Jenny a Chinese doctor with good success. Then I had to have a small growth dug out of my thigh, followed by another on my head. Oh, and I'm not finished yet, as I am writing this, I am waiting an operation for a hernia, this will involve a mesh implant I am told. Mind you I've made a lot of good friends in the hospital Doctors, nurses, paramedics etc so that's one good thing to come out of all this.

(Me on one of my last gigs)

(Andy on pedal steel)

(Lassie in front garden with home-made caravans)

During all this Nan had a bad fall and was hospitalised. When she got out, she was far too much work for the carers as she had to be hoisted everywhere, her dementia was getting worse and i had to put her in a home where she is very well looked after. She knows me and she is quite bright most of the time, but when i ask her does anyone come to see her she says no, but i know that people do visit her she has no shortage of friends. I never told her about Dot and she does ask for her and thinks that she not well, but I tell her she's ok. Someday she doesn't ask for Dot, but yesterday she asked and said she would like to go and see her, what could I say, some people say you should tell her and maybe they are right, and other people say your best not to, she would forget in five minutes anyway and then she would ask again. Her psychiatrist said to me "look Jim I think you're doing the right thing, I would not tell her myself". So that made me feel better but it's hard when Nan asks for Dot and sometimes feel like breaking down and telling her, but I've got to keep strong on this one.

Since I lost my wife Dot, I've found it increasingly hard but not impossible to cope especially if Rory gets flare ups and various other ailments. Going back to the Jacobite I don't know how i would cope at all if they weren't next door. I like the company knowing that there is always someone there it takes a whole lot of pressure off me as it keeps Rory very occupied as that is his whole life and interest. He would be totally lost without Loch Ness by Jacobite the whole crew from Freda the director downwards office staff, ship crew, bus drivers and workers are all so kind and thoughtful to him. Freda has a booming business here and very well deserved for such a nice lady. Wherever you are reading this from i would highly recommend a wee visit and book a nice relaxing trip on one of the four luxury boats. I'm sure you would certainly enjoy it. This next bit is out off context as I find myself remembering things as I go along, but I feel I will just leave it, rather than muddle up the whole story.

Aye times were very hard on the croft when i was young. There was no wage coming into the house, when my dad was not dragging wood with the horse. I remember giving scraps to my dog Rover under the table (a bad habit i must admit) and my dad saying "never mind giving your meat to the dog, grub will be in short supply soon". He knew there were hard times ahead. If it were not for the rabbits, i suppose we would be very, very hungry. I won't say starving because we highland crofters always got by. Living off the land as best we could. We always or nearly always had tatties and tatties and milk was a favourite meal of mine. Nice dry fluffy Kerris pink or Golden wonder tatties mashed in with fresh cow's milk and just enough salt to taste. Rabbit stew, I never gave it a thought it was just like chicken and part of the daily food chain. Well not every day but as long as there were rabbits, we were sure of a meal. Dad used to snare the rabbits and i would go around with him and watched as he gave them a quick chop on the back of the neck. I was often hoping he would let them go, but I do remember once he was just about to deliver the "coup de grace" when he said "ach boy, it's a bit small this one" and he let it go. Dad would gut them, string them in pairs and take them to MacLennan the butchers in the market. They were famed far and near for their sliced sausage and a rabbit or two paid for a nice block of this luxury. The rest of the money was put towards the groceries bread, sugar, tea etc. Maybe ten to fifteen shillings 50p to 70p new money. Ten bob usually paid the grocers van that came round. Poor mum there was never anything left over or very rarely for a pair of nylon stockings. As i said before, my dad was a great piper. He was the Baroness Burtons personal piper and played for her when required. He treasured his bagpipes more than anything they were handed down from his late dad. When we lived at Meikle Ussie I was only two years old but mum told me that the house we lived in went on fire, dad came dashing in from the fields, shouting "the pipes, the pipes, my father's pipes" and he rushed in and managed to rescue them. My mum was laughing when she told me, that was all your dad thought about, saving his father's bagpipes. So, I am sure you will all understand the next story. When we moved from Wester Blackfold to Lower Dunain my dad had managed to build up a few more head of cattle. The calves were penned in the byre and hand reared, but some of the calves were taking ill and eventually one died. Mr Riggs the vet was called out and he took the dead calf away to the laboratory for a post mortem and he came back next day with the news that the calf had died from lead poisoning. My dad said "that's impossible there's no lead about here" and he dismissed it as a bad diagnosis. A second calf died and it was taken to Drummond hill for a post mortem, but with the same diagnosis. My dad said to Mr. Riggs "i can't understand it, i can assure you there's no way these calves have access to any lead products" then suddenly Mr. Riggs turned to dad and said "look there's your problem" the calves pens were made up of old house doors, and here was one of the calves chewing and sucking on the edge of the doors. Flaky old lead paint that was the culprit. So those doors were very quickly taken away and burnt. During this time my dad said "that's us we're finished, there'll be no more calves to sell come market time. I'll just have to sell the bagpipes". Hard and all as my dad was i knew that would have broken his heart. Somehow mum and dad weathered the storm. My dad had a cousin (my Aunty Nan) who were very close to each other, this stemmed from the fact that they were both practically brought up together at Ballymore, Blackfold. Aunty Nan had long since left the unforgiving hardships of Blackfold for the more serene climate of the English countryside. Seven Oaks in Kent, where she married and settled down. Round about the time of our losing the calves, Aunty Nan came up from Kent to pay a visit. I just loved to see her when she came, the most beautiful of women, always so smart, lovely costume, wide brimmed feather hat, court shoes etc. A stark contrast to my poor mum with all the countryside beauty of her rags. But everything stopped when aunty Nan came, work ceased for a while the most important person ever to visit the croft had arrived and a lot of important persons did cross our threshold, a lot before my time. I remember dad throwing the pitchfork down and telling mum to go and put the kettle on. During the course of the ensuing conversation, the subject of the poisoned calves and the sorry state of affairs arose. I remember aunty Nan picking up her big blue handbag, pulling out two £5 notes. Through much argument she pressed the notes into my dad's hand and she said "look Alick take them and I don't want them back, I'm pretty sure that aunty Nan saved the day for us all. The rent had to be paid and that was the princely sum of £5 which was a lot of money back then, more so if you had no immediate way of raising it. One fiver was put to immediate use and the other was put in an old purse under my bed, for a rainy day. Looking back there were many rainy days. My sister Nan who is four years older than I, was definitely the apple of my dad's eye. She was always trying to get me into trouble with dad. My dad was going to teach me to play the bagpipes to keep up the family tradition and he bought me a practice chanter, so after supper every night I would take the chanter out and sit opposite my dad at the table. As I said before he was very hard on me and the least mistake, I made I was shouted at with something like "that's not the way I showed you boy, just do as your told". But some nights, well most nights, somebody would sit in the corner facing me, but out of dads view and pull funny faces at me just to make me laugh, aye that was my big sister Nan. Of course, I was prone to laughing anyway. I don't know why because most of the time I had nothing to laugh about. Sometimes my dad would give me a slap across the ears or as he would sometimes say "I'll warm your lugs for you, what are you laughing at" and of course the laughter turned to crying and that would be the lesson over for the night. That was the last night I took the chanter out, I was too afraid to play it when

Nan was about. I still blame Nan for not learning the bagpipes. I've still got the chanter and dads precious bagpipes and even at 74 it would not take much to persuade me to learn them again.

Well maybe.

(Dad's granny with his cousin Annie Ballymore)

(Johnny next door in the background)

On reflection I know my dad was hard on me, but he must have saved long and hard to but a chanter for me and it wasn't a cheap one it was a top of the range "Hardie" chanter.

I don't want to go on about Nan, for she turned out to be a fine woman, but when she was younger if she wasn't tormenting me she was tormenting the cows, a right Beryl the Peril. One of our cows was called Polly and Nan used to try and jump on her back. She would catch her tail and pull; the poor cow was demented. Turning around first one way and then the other, trying to box Nan with her head. But guess who was standing in the way, one day an innocent bystander ("aye nothing ever goes right for you Jimuck!") Aye that's right little old me although only seven or eight at the time I still remember this very vividly. As Polly swung round, she couldn't reach Nan who was still hanging onto her tail, she made a wild lunge at me and head butted me into the gutters just beside the midding or dunghill. It was this softish landing that probably saved my life, the cow was pushing me into the muck and butting me with her head and I could see the wild glare in her eyes. Nan had let go by this time and the cow now vented her full fury on me. Nan was shouting for help; my dad must have been working close by as he came running over the field and chased Polly away. I can't remember exactly what happened next as I was in a severe state of shock. I had been gored to within an inch of my life. Dad would have asked Nan what happened and i can almost bet that she would have said James was tormenting the cow, but dad got such a fright that there was no more said about it. I seem to remember that we had to get rid of the cow as she was now thought to be too dangerous to have about. Poor Polly, she used to be a lovely docile beast, but even animals have a breaking point. Nan changed her attitude to me, the first time i remember Nan changing her attitude towards me, the path from Blackfold to school ran alongside a treacherous deep rocky gorge over 100ft deep and deeper in places. My dad never tired of warning me to stay away from the rocks. People had moved in next door half a mile away, during our last two years at Blackfold. One of the children was a right clype, I could never understand and still don't know why people were always clyping on me. This day my sister Nan and Maureen our new neighbour was walking ahead of me. I remember shouting to them; I'm going to crawl to the edge to see how deep the gorge is. I crept a wee bit closer and I could see and hear the waters plunging and flowing over the rock's way down many feet below. I didn't think I was that close to the edge. Next day when Nan and i were in the house together, dad said "was James looking over the rocks yesterday" sheer terror filled my wee body and do you know what Nan said "no dad he wasn't" I couldn't believe my "lugs" Maureen had obviously told her mother and she had told my dad of course i still got a stern warning, so I was in a no-win situation.

It's funny how some things come about in this world sometimes. One day i was looking at my electricity bill, i thought they were on the high side so I rang the electricity supplier and asked if they could help with a cheaper tariff or some other solution. The man on the phone was very helpful and we came to a deal. I didn't know this gentleman but what he told me next over the phone quite stunned me, he said "I know someone that knows you an old long lost friend and he has been trying to find you" he said "there's not a day passes when I'm in his company that he doesn't speak of you" he's always going on about his old pal Jim and the great times you had together. The electricity man had remembered Jim's address at Dochgarroch and of course when he saw mine, he put two and two together. He gave me Jim's address in Fort William, he hadn't got his telephone number. Well, I sat down that night and wrote to Jim, my long-lost pal. As i said previously he had left his home to join the RAF many moons ago I could travel round the world ten times and then back, but I would still never ever meet such a loyal, true faithful pal as Jim. We developed a friendship a sort of David and Johnathan thing. We shared a great love for boxing and we used to spar a lot, we made up gloves out of any material we could find rubber hot water bottles were top notch. We fought together, we played badminton together. We laughed together, we sang together we sang and danced together, we loved together and we cried together. At the weekends we would meet up at the local shop with our racing bikes and head off to wherever took our fancy, usually to the hill's miles and miles of open road. Blackfold with all the steep braes was a usual jaunt. It was a sad tearful day when at last Jim got his RAF papers and we bid each other farewell. With the oh so forgotten promise to keeping in touch. It seemed ever so strange when Jim was gone, travelling the roads on my own no sound of the ringing of laughter in my ears or sometimes stop Jim I've got a puncture. However, it wasn't long after that, that i met the first great love of my life and i wasn't alone anymore. A most gorgeous looking girl who everyone seemed to be chasing after chose me out of them all to be her steady. Pat had a driving license which I hadn't got at the time and she had a super red vespa scooter, she used to take me everywhere on it, pick me up from work and then the glorious weekend s. She would get her dads car take us to wherever we wanted to go. The dances at the Strath pavilion were among our favourites. When her dad needed the car Pat would ask for the old civil defense land rover and the big chief told her just to take it. Of course, i was still young then and in my late teens and i used to sneak out of the house and meet her at the top of the road. I often wonder what she thought of me not letting her drive up to my house, of course coming home was different, the dawn was usually breaking by that time. Those were the happiest days of my life. In her arms i felt so secure, so happy and wanted, just to be a man. Not being shouted at all the time or just being taken for granted. Yes, very happy times. We went together for nigh on two years, but i never popped the question. I was still too shy and afraid of what dad would have to say about it. I know he would have said "there's time enough for that loon" I'd heard him say that before. Pat was a tad older than me and maybe she got fed up waiting for me to ask for her hand, or maybe the opposite she might not have wanted to settle down and felt that things were leading that way. However, I'll never know but I'm forever grateful for the happy years we had together and which I will never forget. Pat's job involved her going away on business trips to London and other parts and it was during those times that we drifted apart and now I had lost the two best friends I ever had. Oh, would nothing ever go right for me. I've wandered away a wee bit here, but however one day a knock came on the door and who was standing on the doorstep but my old pal Jim, a wee bit rounder than when I had last seen him over forty-five years ago. But the same old happy go lucky Jim. We stood and looked at each other for ages it seemed, and then we threw our arms around each other and enjoyed the moment of the reunion.

The two Jim's were together again and oh what stories we had to tell each other. Jim told me later that day, that he had a bit of a job holding himself together and I had to admit so had I. Since then, we keep in close contact and we enjoy exchanging our yarns.

Just at the foot of Blackfold Brae lived my Grand Uncle Danny. He dwelt in a lovely little wooden cabin tucked into the edge of a tall forest of larchen trees. A crooked narrow path led up to it with ivy covered stone walls either side. The cabin had the most amazing view of the valley stretching out below and looking onto the far away. Monaliadh Mountain range. Nobody ever passed the cabin without commenting on such a beautiful place to build a house. Jamie my son, who does the Royal mail round at Blackfold often stops at the layby opposite the manny in the braes gateway to have his sandwich. One day he said to me "see if I ever come into money, I know where I would love to build a house", Before he said anymore I knew exactly the place he was talking about.

Uncle Danny was known to one and all as the "manny in the brae" my dad and i would sometimes see him in his garden as we walked home and I remember my dad saying "do you not get lonely there at nights living all on your own, you could come and stay with us we have plenty room" "Ouch no" said Danny I'm fine here, I've got the "Roosers" to keep me company. My dad said "don't talk such nonsense" Danny replied "it's not nonsense the Roosers live among the trees, they keep me company at night". Dad must have known who the roosers were for he said "sheesht man don't frighten the loon' 'but he kept on about the Roosers. I kept on asking dad who or what the Roosers were but he never ever told me, i guess i'll never know. One night his little wood cabin caught fire and try as he might the manny in the brae could not save his humble abode as he stood and watched it burn to the ground. He made himself a crude little shelter with some old sheets of corrugated iron he had rescued from the ashes. Eventually the manny in the Brae was persuaded by my dad to come and live with us, but he was never happy although extremely grateful. The lure of his old little cabin with its majestic views, although no longer there kept pulling on his heartstrings and he went home. Blackfold was a cold unforgiving place, especially in winter which was fast approaching and we all worried about my uncle Danny. One bitter cold winter morning, Kenny Chisholm the postie called with one of his twice weekly rounds of mail. He had a sombre look on his face that told it all. He said to my dad "I called into see the manny in the brae and i found him lying in his wee shelter frozen to death, partially covered by the snow that had drifted in". The wind was whistling through the tall larch trees as they swayed to and fro just as if the Roosers were mourning the passing of their old companion. Every time I go to Blackfold i just stop outside where his little cabin once stood. There is nothing now left to be seen, but the path leading up through the two ivy covered walls is still there as if it has been meticulously cared for since Danny passed away. I wonder do the Roosers get lonely without him.

As i said before Blackfold was notorious for snow fall and blizzards especially in the forties and fifties. For some reason we don't seem to get these severe winters quite as often or if ever. I recall quite vividly one day setting off for school on a mild winter morning, early afternoon a storm arose and my school closing time it was a white out and that was on the lower ground. During this time our next-door neighbour a Mrs. Macdonald had adopted three orphan children Mary, Donny and Kenny she had a daughter of her own Maureen. They were all with me that afternoon as well as my sister Nan and Billy Ross the gamekeeper's son who hadn't so far to go as the rest of us. Darkness was fast descending as we left the warmth of our little country school at Dochgarroch and into the bitter winter cold. I couldn't have been more than eight years old as my sister Nan was still with us in primary school and she was four years older than i. I was wearing short trousers and the further we climbed the deeper was the snow, it was well over my knees in places. I was struggling a wee bit to keep up with the older children but I kept going on hindsight to stop would have almost certainly been fatal. I remember shouting to them in front that my socks were frozen. They were caked in ice and sticking to me. We reached Ballymore which was near the summit of Blackfold and there we parted company with Billy the gamekeeper's son, I could see the warm welcome light as his mum opened the door and smelled the unmistakable smell of the peat fire. Well, that was Billy home but we had another mile or two to go yet. I remember telling Nan to stop for a rest, but she said no, she being older had the sense not to stop." If we stop, we will freeze to death" she said. The snow was getting deeper and deeper and by now it was blowing a gale and drifting some of the drifts were waist deep. As we approached the peak of the hill, we could just see through the blizzard the lights of Maggie and Lexy's log cabin. The sparks and the grey smoke ascending up to the heavens was a cheering sight. Another mile to go God willing and we would be home. We reached Lexy's cabin and just next door was Mrs. MacDonald's house where the three orphans and Maureen lived. That just left Nan and I and on we went, but for the tracks that Nan made ahead of me I would have perished that night. Many a soul would have perished by the grace of God and his guiding hand we made it. We were home, we rushed in through the door to a big roaring fire, the tilly lamp and candles set the room aglow. My mum grabbed me in her arms and hugged me. Then she said to my dad "Alick I can't get James socks off they're frozen solid" mum went through to get some hot water and dad shouted "no, no woman do you want him to lose his legs. Dip them in cold water "I don't know how long mum was getting my socks off as I couldn't feel anything, my legs were numb you could have cut them off they were void of all feeling. When she did get them off, they were bleeding, my skin was cracking and open. I remember dad saying "oh boy, he's got frostbite" then at last i was wrapped up in a warm blanket as mum tried to restore some feeling into my legs. I can't remember much after that or how the rest of my body coped, but I'm sure we all went back to school when the blizzards past.

(Johnny next door with milk cow)

Wedding at one of Lexy's barns) Mid-sixties I think it was, my grandad who had been staying in Blackfold with his daughter's aunty Belle came to live with us. This was a great help to mum, he was a really good chef and he did all the cooking he also helped out immensely with the grocery's stovies, stews, fry ups, soups and his specialty clouty dumplings I Poor mum she wouldn't know whether to laugh or cry when she would come into the house sometimes and say "I think grandads made another of his dumplings" you could hardly see a yard in front of you for steam which had melted the wallpaper paste The ceiling wallpaper especially was hanging down almost touching the table, but then mum would get the floor brush and push it all back in place again. The paste was made of flour in the old days. When I came in grandad would wink at me and look through his fast dimming hazy blue eyes and say, "James I've got a treat for you tonight I've made a dumpling' 'I kidded on I didn't know despite all the evidence hanging about me. but all this cooking grandad did mean more time working out in the fields for mum. she hadn't to rush home to make the supper and rush back out so often. We always had to go back out to work after supper.

Grandad was a tough wizened man a very, very kind man. he was very good to me and made my life a lot easier, he would notice when I hadn't got a smoke and he would throw me a 20 rack of cigarettes. He told me he was born in Liverpool and he was one of 12 of a family. His parents were a rough and ready crew and could not afford to feed them, nor could they be bothered with them and they were all thrown out onto the streets to fend for themselves. He never saw his brothers and sisters again.

He had no decent clothes as one can imagine and most of his clothes were adult throwaways which helps explain the next bit. He went down to the Liverpool docks and applied for a job as cabin boy on a merchant schooner. It was then that he changed his name to O'Neil. He thought that with an Irish sounding name he would be more likely to get work as the Irish were noted good hard workers. The captain of the skipper weighed grandad up and down and asked him how old he was. grandad pulled his cap down a wee bit and told him he was sixteen although he was only twelve. after another few questions, the skipper said "ok I'll takes you on as our cabin boy, preparing meats for the crew and all other housekeeping jobs.

His first trip was to South America and then he told me this "James" he said, "I was up the Amazon river when I was twelve". They were trading with the Amazon Indians who lived along the banks of the river most were friendly but there were some remote tribes who you would steer a wide berth of. He told me a lot of stories, but as my old school teacher Mrs. McFadyen used to say, it went in one ear and out the other. and another fact that grandad was quite proud of was that he had black blood in him, while on one of his trips he had a horrific accident and he needed a blood transfusion. Seemingly the only blood that was available was from a black donor and he was always forever grateful to that man for saving his life. Grandad and granny lived apart for a good part of their lives as Grandad was away at sea for long periods, when WW11 started he served as chief stoker on the destroyer H.M.S TIGER. He must have been some character in his youth. He was always promising granny he'd be coming home on leave and granny would post some money to him to help him with his fare when he got ashore, but mostly he never came home. The lure of the sea was in his blood and he was forever grateful to it for taking him away from the Liverpool slums. Sometimes he would gaze into the fire and start telling the stories about his mis spent youth but considering all he went through i think he did very well for himself. I wonder how his brothers and sisters fared; I would dearly love to know. "James" he said "I'm lucky to be here" I suppose he liked a good tipple, rum probably. "one night in Singapore I was staggering along the wooden dock and someone had left one of the floor hatches open, I fell straight through the open hatch to the water some twenty feet below. But by good luck there was a small rowing boat moored under the dock with a small cargo of cotton bales and i landed right on top of them". Was it not for the rowing boat he would most surely have drowned, especially with the drunken state he was in.?

Eventually he left the sea, this must have broken his heart and he got a job as boilerman with the UK atomic energy factory at Preston just outside Blackpool with his daughter and aunty Belle and Uncle Jack.

A real character who was on the go back then was nicknamed "Santa" by the locals. He was our neighbour for a while at Dunain but he seemed to let himself go, He turned very eccentric and whimsical as he grew older. He was very well known around town. One day I was sitting in the dentists waiting room and who walked in but Santa. Long white beard a big mop of white hair sticking out from under his battered and beaten trilby hat and wellington boots to match. He strode up to the reception desk and rang the bell, he told the receptionist that he had a bad tooth and wanted an extraction. The lady said "I'm sorry but you will need an appointment as we are totally booked today". The lady told Santa that there was a chap Matheson who might help him, Santa replied "it's a dentist i want not a flipping plumber". (Matheson was also the name of a well-known plumber in town). At last, the receptionist told Santa to take a seat and she would go and see if she could help. It was just then that he spotted me and started asking me all the questions of the day, like was i still busking in the bars and did i know old Macdonald had a farm and with that he burst into song. There were quite a few in the waiting room and Santa was enjoying all the attention he was getting and he sang that much louder. Oh boy was i glad when it was my turn to be seen. Thankfully when i got out he was gone. Shortly after this word went around town that Santa had got himself a car as he was seen travelling into town in this big posh car and they didn't think he had a driving license. It so transpired that someone get a right close up and noticed Santa had his welly boots up on the dash, it was a left-hand drive car and some holiday maker had given him a lift into town so he was obviously a passenger in the right-hand seat.

We never got much at Christmas, but i remember one-time Nan and I were upstairs in bed, our beds were opposite each other and mum came in with an apple and a banana. Of course, Nan grabbed the banana, i had never seen a banana before let alone tasted one. I pestered her asking to swap the apple for the banana, but she would not swap. I told her I didn't want the apple mum was going to give me the banana but you grabbed it off her. "ok" Nan said "you throw the apple over and I'll throw the banana over" so I threw the apple over gee whizz did it not hit her in the eye or so she said, she then started crying "I'm telling daddy on you, you'll get it" I started pleading with her please don't tell dad, you can have my apple as well. She nipped out of bed (i found this out later) went downstairs to mums' lipstick and painted her eye red with mum's lipstick. She came back upstairs and said "look at that it's bleeding I'll need to get the doctor" it was my mum who persuaded Nan not to tell dad as she noticed that Nan had used her lipstick and that was the end of that, but as far as i can remember. It was a long time before I found out what a banana tasted like.

As time went by Nan lost her childish attitude towards me and the next story, I'm about to tell you i find most embarrassing. It was Christmas day 1955 and i was eleven years old. I woke Christmas day morning and there were no presents to be seen anywhere. I knew we never got much but there was always a little something. Nan came over and threw her arms around me and said "what's wrong James, why are you crying? 'I said Santa never came, Nan said "you still don't believe in Santa, there's no such thing as Santa". No one told me it was a well-kept secret all my eleven years. Imagine believing in Santa at that age. However, Nan was four years older than I was and she never ever told me. I remember the sheer disappointment of coming to terms with the fact that Santa didn't exist. Nan went to her handbag and pulled out her purse and she filled my eager trembling hands with a pile of loose change. Threepenny pieces, tanners, shillings, penny's the lot. This just goes to show how the older kids kept Santa a secret back then. We were warned not to tell the young ones otherwise.

Andy's dad Ian Kennedy always used to say "what a cruel thing the Santa Claus tale was, telling your kids about him and then one day watching their castles come tumbling down when they discover that there's no Santa. You see i was brought up to always tell the truth and never speak lies, so everything i was told i thought was true no matter who or what it was. This is reflected in the next story. Dennis "the spear man" and I were walking along the high street one day this guy with a Glasgow spoken accent stopped us and jarred us for a shilling for the bus to Beauly. Dennis didn't entertain him; he was street wise not like me a green country yokel just down from the hills for a day. The guy turned to me and asked me for a shilling for the fare to Beauly "there must be an awful lot of people going to Beauly" I thought. "It's ok" he said "I'll pay you back, I'll meet you here at 11 o'clock Monday morning and I'll give you your shilling back". So, I gave him the shilling. Dennis looked at me in awe as the guy turned around and walked away, he said "you know you'll never see that guy again" I said to Dennis I will he promised me he would meet me here Monday at 11 o'clock. Dennis started laughing, even he could not believe how green I was. Looking back, I can't believe it myself. I wonder did the guy turn up on Monday.

(Dochgarroch school children at Christmas party, Baroness Burton and Major Mellis standing at the rear right)

Due to my being brought up in the hills of Blackfold in my early days there were no other kids to play with I was a very shy person and I suppose I still am. Back then I was never used to company and I would shy away from people. With this in mind I remember one day after school at Dochgarroch, we were all hanging about, waiting to make our various ways home. Two of the older boys picked on a much younger girl Cathy Macdonald, I remember her name quite vividly. This big bully Robert dug a piece of wood into the ditch and scooped up a spoonful of muck and gutters. His mate grabbed Cathy and said "eat that" and he jammed it into her mouth, Cathy started crying and all the other kids were laughing. I was only about eight at the time but i remember very well as clear as daylight going over to her taking her hand and saying "Never mind Cathy, take my hand and come with me" there was silence the bully's said nothing, i can't remember being frightened as we walked up the road Cathy and I. Next night at the same spot we heard this loud shout from just around the corner at the top of the brae. It was Cathy's big brother "you leave my wee sister alone or I'll come down there and I'll belt the lot of you" and poor Cathy was left in peace after that. Cathy left Dochgarroch school shortly after that, her parents must have moved on and I never saw her again. I often think of her and wonder how she got on in life and if she is still around and if she is, does she remember the wee boy who took her hand that day many, many moons ago. Now if Cath turned up on my doorstep wouldn't that be some surprise.

One of Lexy's relations was a very famous character he was called Jock the swapper known throughout the whole of Blackfold, Abriachan and beyond. I remember my dad and other locals talking about him, he wore a long bushy red beard. Those beards seemed to be quite common in those days, Jock lived on a croft just past Loch Laide on the Blackfold, Abriachan road. Amongst other things, Jock was famously notorious for making his own moonshine, or the illicit whiskey. There were a lot of people at it in the hills, but Jocks special blend had gained him a great reputation it tasted and kicked like no other. The banning of making the moonshine was imposed upon us after the battle of Culloden in an effort to suppress the wild highland clansman. I myself totally disagree with this imposition as many a Highlander supported his family with the sales thereof. The customs and <u>excise</u> knew that Jock was at it and they tried their darndest to catch him, but he was always a step or two or maybe three ahead of them. Jock kept shifting his still from place to place. It wasn't a great big piece of apparatus; it was like a giant copper kettle with a large funnel attached. I remember seeing one in Johnny next doors barn. One story goes that he had a really wild garron and nobody could get past this horse except Jock himself. He had the horse tied up in its stall and you could just manage to squeeze past it into the shed next door where he kept his still. One day the customs having got wind that the still was in the stable visited Jock, but they couldn't get past the garron or they would be kicked to death. Jock refused to shift it saying to them that he was just as likely to be kicked as they were. They said to Jock "don't worry we'll be back better prepared", but by the time they returned Jock had relocated his apparatus and blotted out all traces of his moonshine activity. He once had quite a large order for the Bogroy Inn, just a few miles over the hill. But Jock got wind that the customs were hot on his trail, i think there must have been a small reward out for him. Jock sent a messenger down to Inverness to order two taxis or carriages and he managed to get information to the customs that Jock the "swapper" would be carrying a cargo of moonshine in a certain carriage at a certain time to the Bogroy Inn. Jock sat in the first carriage by himself after loading his moonshine into the second carriage, the customs were lying in wait as Jock's taxi came into view and he was stopped by customs. "We've got you this time Jock" they said as they started a search of the vehicle. And in the meantime, amongst all the kerfuffle that Jock was creating the second carriage sailed on by practically unnoticed and delivered Jock's moonshine to the Inn. Once again, the customs were foiled, i don't think they ever pinned anything on him. On another note, during the winters Jocks <u>corn stooks</u> or at least a few of them were left out. Passersby used to remark how lazy and stupid Jock was for leaving his stooks out all winter, but what they didn't know was that Jock had snares set in amongst the sheaves and the pheasants would come in for a feed of corn only to be trapped in Jocks snares. Jock must have done fairly well with his pheasants and moonshine. A way of life long gone.

I couldn't possibly leave this account of the Loch Ness monster out of my book as related by my late dear mum which she told to many people who visited. The old main road prior to 1939 ran from Inverness to Drumnadrochit taking a route which passed by just at the back of the old croft house at Lower Dunain. When she was just a wee lassie she would see all the people making their way home from a day in town and the crofters going home from the cattle sales in their pony and trap and horse carts. The road is still there but is broken up in places by cattle fences and field extensions. Sometimes they would stop for a blether and old aunty Belle would ask them in for a cup of tea, a bit of craic and a wee tune on her melodeon. Several people told aunt Belle about the monster on different occasions it was seen crossing the road ahead of them with a sheep in its mouth. These were God fearing people, my aunt Belle included and had no reason whatsoever to make up a false account.

In those days there was no traffic on the road to frighten the monster, unlike today with all the heavy traffic and the new road blasted out. of the rock has formed an instrumental barrier high above the waters. I recall these stories very vividly they seem to be incarcerated in the depths of my mind. While on the subject of the monster an old workmate of mine had a really frightening experience on the loch. I remember it well it was on M.F.R radio that i first heard the account. I hadn't seen Ian for a long, long time apart from a fleeting glimpse, but i decided to dig him up and he gave me some newspaper cuttings, a DVD which was made by a French company and here follows Ian's story.

The following is an account of a sighting of the Loch Ness monster given by an old friend and work companion of mine and printed in a local newspaper dated 14/07/1976.

Two Inverness mechanics who were testing a boat

on Loch Ness said yesterday they had been surrounded by "Monsters" they described how they had watched in fear and amazement as five large humps weaved around their delicate craft for a full fifteen minutes. "It was like getting caught in a school of whales' 'said Mr. Ian Dunn (29) of 154 Old town road, Inverness "we were so afraid they might overturn the boat that we put on our life jackets. We were frightened but we were also fascinated it was just fantastic, I only half believed the stories before so many people have seen something and i thought there may be something in it. But you have got to see it to believe it" he explained. "We didn't have a camera, the hooter on the boat was broken and we didn't have any flare, so we couldn't attract anyone's attention, it wouldn't have made any difference anyway, the view from the road would have been hidden by the trees".

Mr. Dunn, service manager of a local garage and

Mr. Billy Kennedy (28) of 14 Crown Avenue, Inverness had repaired a friend's boat and were testing it near Abriachan pier on Monday Evening.

"We were cruising along about quarter throttle when I turned around to look at the wake and saw five humps, all in a line I called to Billy and they broke away, moving through the water separately. I could hardly believe what I saw, I've never experienced anything like it before. We are out twice a week on the Loch and we've also been deep sea fishing. The Loch was like a mirror and it was morning. We decided to go back for a closer look and once we were among them it was very eerie, we were almost on top of them". He described the humps as matt black in colour, about eight feet long and about three feet high pyramid shape but rounded on top. "Sometimes the humps would disappear below the surface, we never knew where they would come up again, that was what was so frightening. They weren't scared of the sound of our engine when we pulled away one of them followed us".

Mr. Kennedy said "I didn't believe in the Loch Ness Monster before but I'm inclined to believe it now. I don't know what we saw, we could only make out the humps but they were definitely not seals, they were too big and if they had been seals, we would have seen their heads.

(Dot and I last waltz)

(Dot in happy times)

(My mum and Jamie)

Since my wife passed away in May 2017, Life suddenly took a different route. Gone were all the arguments and then the making up that always followed, gone were all the sharing of tasks and chores, the looking after and taking care of Rory, which at times when his eczema and his other problems were at a high was a monumental task, patience and endurance were pushed to the very limit, aye and sometimes beyond. I was now on my own I was struggling for a while for I had my own problems to contend with. I had plastic surgery operations on my scalp for skin cancers, also on my thigh, carpel tunnel operations on my wrists. Then on top of it all my sister Nan was starting to wonder at night, the early signs of dementia, which she was diagnosed with shortly after. I had to look after Nan with daily visits, making sure she had plenty to eat and drink. I didn't know what she was doing with all the bread I took up to her, two loaves at a time and every day she would say "it's a good job you came up today I've no bread left". I had to see the funny side of it, she must have been feeding the birds. Eventually I had to get carers in, four visits a day, which was a big relief to me although I still had to make sure there were meals in the house for her, plus all the other necessaries. Nan had two bad falls in the house, which resulted in two bone fractures and eventually she was too much of a handful for the carers and I and after several months in hospital she was admitted to Highview nursing home.

During this time Miss Freda Newton owner of Jacobite Cruises and now our next-door neighbour was doing up and extending the old village memorial hall with a view to turning it into a gift shop and restaurant. The old hall was totally refurbished and practically a mirror image was built alongside, with a paved courtyard in-between. It is now finished and it is a magnificent building indeed and with it just being a couple of stone's throw away from my house, I find myself wandering down midafternoons Rory and I for coffees and apple juice. It didn't take us long for us to get to know all the staff, ever so friendly and efficient. I really enjoy getting out of the house, meeting people and getting the craic. All the loneliness of Blackfold now seem a million miles away.

Just recently I got a phone call from my cousin Liz, who moved up from Seven Oaks, Kent to live in Nairn, telling me that she was in the An Talla with her brother Alec whom I had not seen for sixty years and his partner Mark. We talked and reminisced over cups of coffee about Blackfold, Maggie, Lexy, Nellie, Ghosts and all the rest. Liz told me again as she had done many times before that she had seen a ghost at Blackfold. Well, she said if there is any place on earth you would likely see a ghost it would be Blackfold. Mark and I seemed to hit it off right away. He was intrigued by the stories and when I told him about this book, he said he would have to buy one he was fascinated by it all. Culloden was mentioned and here was I surrounded by three English people. Mark looked at me and with his cockney accent and a wide beaming grin he said "look Jim if I had a choice whose side, I would fight in it would be for the Scots". I thought that priceless.

On the Sixth September 2019 the Bronze war memorial plaque was unveiled. It was quite a large poignant ceremony. The British Legion were there with their standard bearers a lone piper played and the last post was sounded. The Lord Lieutenant was there with members of the armed forces and I had the honour of laying one of the wreaths representing the local community. There are people commemorated on the plaque and after all those years since the war they are remembered in bronze for all to see and not hidden away in some dimly lit obscure hall. My sincere thanks and gratitude to Freda and Douglas for this magnificent gesture. I would dearly love to find out what happened to Johnny Dunain and will try and make a last effort to find out. After all he gave his life for me and my people and I should not forget him. Ach well that maybe my next book, the Lord willing. "What happened to Johnny Dunain".

Another person I met and got to know was Douglas Yule, a friend of Freda's. Douglas was doing some research into some of the names on the plaque and when he was doing the research on Johnny Dunain who was the same bloodline as myself, he came up with some amazing findings. I don't quite know how he managed this but he traced my family tree back to my great great great great Grandmother who wore this tartan dress which currently lives in the Inverness Museum.

(Great Grandmothers dress)

With the hall being a memorial hall, there was a wooden plaque on one of the inside walls commemorating the locals who had fallen and given their lives in the second world war. To her great credit and thoughtfulness. Freda has rescued the plaque and has had a beautiful bronze one made to replace the old wooden one, a magnificent gesture. The bronze plaque will be fixed to a large headstone on the outside gable wall of the old hall for all to see. My grand uncle Johnny Dunain is one of several mentioned on the plaque and I have Freda to thank for although Johnny Dunain's body to my knowledge was never found, reported missing his name will live on in bronze and never be forgotten.

I am finding it quite difficult to finally bring an end to my story as I feel maybe I have left so much out, but before I close I think it would be so nice and only right that having talked about all my old friends and acquaintances, that I should give a mention to some of my new friends that have endeared themselves to me. They all seem to have so much time for Rory and I which makes me feel to say the least, not so lonely and on my own maybe even wanted once again. I find myself drawn like a magnet to An Talla, after all or well mostly all of my chores are done. Ouch I'll cut the grass tomorrow and that pile of ironing, that can wait. I'll just put on my cleanest dirty shirt as Kris Kristofferson would say. Robert the An Talla Manager always makes us welcome as do Gavin Fraser, Robyn Kristina, Becks, Dana and there's Ciorstaidh, now there's a girl and a half she is just made for An Talla, she even makes Rory's dairy free chocolate cake for him. Then a wee mention to the bubbly evanescent Emma, always good for a bit of craic and all the others who have worked there and made us so welcome. Oh and of course there is the really extra special Nicola, a most lovely endearing lassie in every way. So efficient and attentive, I could write a whole chapter on Nicks alone. Her friendship to Rory and I is something special, something I'll cherish for the rest of my life until old father time finally has his way. Sad thing is, they are mostly all students and they go back to university at the end of the season, I will so much miss them all. Getting to close to people just like my mum used to do was always one of my weaknesses, if you can call it that and I just absolutely hate goodbyes. However, I hope and like to think that one sunny day, we will bang into each other somewhere along life's highway and we can enjoy the craic once again.

Well now my dear friends here come a very sad hour or two in my life as I wind down my story and say goodbye to all my dear old past friends and acquaintances. Goodbye to Maggie, Lexy and Ellie. Those three wonderful larger than life characters. Goodbye to Johnny next door who taught me that sound takes time to travel. Goodbye the Mannie in the brae and his ghostly friends and Roozers.

There's no one left now to tell about these wonderful people except me 'the last of the BlackFolders" and soon old father time will catch up with me. I can't run as fast as I used to. Of course, there are a lot of other people no longer with me. My dear mum and dad, uncles, aunts, neighbours and workmates no enemies. I loved them all. And of course, my darling wife Dot. I find even at my age memories never fade or die, they get more golden and more treasured and my mind is a little box to keep them in and I pray I'll never lose the key till it's time for me to hand it over.

When that time comes, I hope to meet up with all of them again. No more blizzards to struggle through no more cancers or diseases. No more dark lonely nights, just happiness being with the Lord. And before I go folks if you feel like telling me how you got on with this book good or bad, I'd sincerely love to hear from you as my mum and I's relations are scattered all over the world, Canada, USA, Australia, New Zealand, HongKong, the Falklands etc. Email jamesfraser100@aol.com

Take care and God Bless
Jim x

High above the shore of Loch Ness over 1,000ft above sea level. Lies a small community of scattered houses, each with their own little croft, Blackfold and this is the place I was brought up in. A mystical place, miles from nowhere and full of ghostly tales and mysterious goings on. Each house had it own unique, very special, very strange characters and as you read on you will meet them all. Each character had their own peculiar way of living on the crofts, a way of life long forgotten and faded away into the misty heathery hillsides. There are all sorts of revelations in this book rom Ghosts to the Loch Ness monster. The hardships of living on the croft and I'll take you right up to the present day through all the changes that have taken place.

Printed and bound by CPI Group (UK) Ltd, Croydon, CR0 4YY